WEAVING

a Spiritual Life

Ann Marie Bezayiff

WEAVING
a Spiritual Life

TATE PUBLISHING & *Enterprises*

Published by Tate Publishing & Enterprises, LLC
127 E. Trade Center Terrace | Mustang, Oklahoma 73064 USA
1.888.361.9473 | www.tatepublishing.com

Tate Publishing is committed to excellence in the publishing industry. The company reflects the philosophy established by the founders, based on Psalm 68:11,
"The Lord gave the word and great was the company of those who published it."

Book design copyright © 2011 by Tate Publishing, LLC. All rights reserved.
Cover design by April Marciszewski
Interior design by Chelsea Womble

Published in the United States of America

ISBN: 978-1-61346-284-3
1. Religion, Christian Life, Devotional
2. Religion, Christian Life, Spiritual Growth
11.08.09

This book is dedicated to Carla Jane Ratliff, my Saturday Sister

ACKNOWLEDGMENTS

Weaving a Spiritual Life is a collection of stories, the words and thoughts woven together from day to day experiences with faith. Working from my weaver's bench, the stories unfolded in the quiet and repetition of my loom, but it was the perseverance and hard work of many others who made this book a possibility.

First, I would like to thank Tate Publishing & Enterprises, for accepting my manuscript, and their staff, who made this book a reality. I'm indebted to my editor, Ashley Luckett, who asked the right questions and challenged me to rethink and rewrite, always rewrite. I owe a special thank you to April Marciszewski and Chelsea Womble for their graphic design work.

I am grateful to the many community members who have supported my writing. A sincere thank you to the members of Grand Avenue United Methodist Church and Trinity Lutheran Church of Porterville, California, for printing my articles of faith. I am thankful for St. Mary's Church in Sanger, where I first heard God's Word. *The Porterville Recorder* newspaper has been instrumental in helping to spread my stories of Christian life in a secular newspaper. Thank you for supporting my column, "From the Olive Orchard."

Thank you to my friends for their comments and

encouragement. Judy Lowery opened the world of writing to me with a simple question: "Would you like to write the church newsletter?" My articles first appeared in her "Good News" column, until I began my own column. Pam, Lorraine, and Mary, your friendships have been a valuable source of energy. Thank you to my siblings—Carla, Jim, Rich, and Tom. I would also like to express my gratitude to Donna Tacchino and other family members.

Nate, Emily, Brian, and Nolan, you are a daily reminder of the love Christ has for his children. David, I owe you so much. Because of your support and love, I have been able to write freely and without constraint. Your constructive comments and gentle feedback have been invaluable.

Thank you, Lord, for all these wonderful people who have come into my life, for their support and patience. Thank you for your guiding hand as this book was formed and fashioned, woven from your Word, for your glory.

TABLE OF CONTENTS

PREFACE

My first-floor loom was a gift from my husband, David. It was a Christmas morning when I found a large, unfamiliar box under the tree. This was unexpected. With scissors and brute strength, the two of us managed to pry open the cumbersome rectangular container amid our children's toys, fallen ornaments, and Christmas stockings. A piece of paper fell out of the box, and I realized that a floor loom was inside. *How can a floor loom fit into a box?* I thought. Then I realized that the individual pieces of the loom were inside. I read those dreaded words, "Assembly required." It was our job to put it together. Not to be deterred, we began sorting and categorizing. By the end of the day, pieces of wood, metal, and leather straps lay in piles all over the living room floor. Another thick book of instructions was the last item out of the box. Like a gigantic jigsaw puzzle, we spent the next week matching and fitting pieces together, and slowly, my loom took shape.

Since then I have been a weaver. What draws me to my weaver's bench is confrontation. It's the challenge of creating a singular piece of fabric out of unrelated fibers, each with its distinct feel, color, and composition. Hopefully my calculations, choices, and vision, combined with a minimal amount of mistakes and miscalculations, form something worthwhile. I become a better weaver as I work through each new project. There are always mistakes, but compared to my first attempts at weaving, they aren't as numerous or noticeable. With experience, I have learned to look for common roadblocks and obstacles, knowing there will be new hurdles to work through.

It's that way with my Christian life. As I prepare or work the loom, I am reminded of my walk with the Lord and the challenges and rewards I experience with each new project in my life's journey. I found weaving and the Christian walk had a strong connection. So the idea of this book formed and took shape as I worked from my weaver's bench.

INTRODUCTION

Just as a weaver works the yarn and creates the fabric, so too are we uniquely woven pieces of art produced from the breath of God. Each thread of our humanity is set in his image. Unlike the human weaver, God's calculations are perfect. There are no mistakes, oversights, or uneven salvages. We are precious and loved because he has formed us.

> For you created my inmost being,
> You knit me together in my
> mother's womb.
> I praise you because I am fearfully
> and wondrously made;
> your works are wonderful,
> I know that full well.
> My frame was not hidden from you
> when I was made in the secret place
> When I was woven together in the
> depths of the earth,
> your eyes saw my unformed body.
> All the days ordained for me
> were written in your book
> before one of them came to be.
>
> Psalm 139:13–16

Ann Marie Bezayiff

Weavers of Christian Life

God created us before our human conception. He designed our bodies and souls; we were part of creation even as the heavens and earth were formed. So too the weaver's beginning is at the end. The finished piece is first created in the mind's eye of the fiber artist. The shape, texture, color, and purpose of the cloth are planned and predetermined before the fingers ever begin their movements. Once the plan is shaped and formed, the weaver works through steps in a long process. Like a complicated recipe, each step is deliberate, measured, and calculated. The investment of time and thought is immeasurable.

Nothing is left to chance; however, sometimes the yarns twist and turn unexpectedly. The salvage ends pull in or stretch out. A single strand of yarn breaks or unravels. A knot unties. Colors, so vibrant in a skein of yarn, become dulled or dingy when woven together. It is as if the piece takes on a will of its own. So even though every step is intentional, sometimes things don't work out as expected. The outcome might be better than anticipated, sometimes different or even a disappointment. That's the nature of weaving and our life experiences as well.

With each experience and with practice the weaver becomes more confident and skillful. Matching the textures and weights of yarns, choosing colors that work well together and anticipating errors become easier. The unexpected becomes the expected. The complexity and intricacy of the process produces a unique piece of art. No one piece is exactly like another. The weaver wouldn't want it any other way. No one human is exactly like another. God didn't want it any other way either.

As we grow and change in our humanity through our physical and spiritual being, we are like these weavers of cloth. Each thread of experience, good or bad, makes the whole piece of our being. The following is a collection of articles and short stories that reflect my thoughts and experiences as I am shaped and woven. The final work is yet to be finished.

STEP 1:

Beginning at the End: Choices and Calculations for a Strong Foundation

Weaving is a step-by-step process, and so is building our relationship with Christ. The first step is creating a strong foundation. In weaving, it's the choice of fiber and the selection of designs and calculations. In our Christian life, it is the desire to have a relationship with Christ, and that begins with spending time with God's Word and in prayer. Faith is required for both!

The first step in weaving is selecting a project. What do you want to make or create on your loom? Will it be a shawl, a set of placemats, a piece of clothing, or an art piece? Will the final project be delicate, soft, pliable, sturdy, or stiff? What shades and hues are envisioned?

The answers depend on the choice of fibers. Some are synthetic, man-made fibers or natural fibers, such as cotton, wool, silk, and linen. Some are dyed with natural plants, while most are factory-colored.

The warp becomes the frame of the piece. Individual ends of the fibers are measured by length and then gathered together and tied down in the front and the back of the loom. Fibers for the warp shouldn't be too thick or heavily textured. Elasticity can be a problem too. Choices need to take into consideration the fineness or coarseness of the project.

The weft fibers or yarns are woven in and out of the stationary warp. The artist has more flexibility when selecting yarn for the weft. These fibers can be heavy, thick, thin, textured, or fragile. Sometimes a final decision simply depends on the feel of the yarn in the artist's hands and a vision of color combinations in the mind.

A NEW SCHOOL YEAR

There is something exciting about the start of a school year. Store displays of new school supplies appear in the middle of July and on into August and September. Neatly stacked boxes of sharpened pencils are just waiting to be opened. A variety of colors and designs are available, so many to choose from, but I prefer the traditional yellow ones. Nearby are stacks of college-ruled lined paper. Crayons are sharp and pointed. They too come in different sizes. Felt pens are bright with color; some are scented and release subtle scents through plastic wrappers. Designer backpacks and insulated lunch bags stock the shelves. Next to them are notebooks, binders, and folders—many of which are covered with Transformers, Spider-Man, or the latest character appearing on cartoons and movies. Others are illustrated with cuddly and cute animals, while some are plain in color or pattern. Many are covered with plastic pockets to hold pictures.

For those who are fortunate, a new outfit is saved for the first day of school. Maybe a pair of new shoes or name-brand shirt. For others, it will be the best outfit they have at the time. Boys will have visited a barber for a fresh haircut, while others might try a new hair style. The night before the first day of school, children and teenagers will have showered or bathed and been sent off to bed early. Some will sleep better than others.

Morning comes quickly, and suddenly, it's the first day of school. Students look forward to seeing friends and renewing last year's friendships. Each student checks out the list of classmates posted outside the office door. Some children question silently, *What will the teacher be like? Will my teacher be nice or mean? Will there be a lot of homework? Will school be too hard? Will I get good grades? Will the teacher like me?*

For others, *Does the teacher know that I got into trouble last year? I hope not because this year I am going to be different. I will turn in all my homework and I won't get into trouble. Will the other kids like me?* Some even pray.

The first day is always filled with anticipation and expectations. It's a day of new beginnings and fresh starts. I feel the same way with each new weaving project. I put aside the difficulties and problems from the last project and begin again, hoping for better results.

Being a Christian is like that too, only we don't have to wait for an exact day or a special time to start over again and to try to become more Christ-like. With Christ, any time is a good time to start a new year. And we don't have to worry about grades; we've already passed. However, it might be the homework that slows us down.

> For all have sinned and fall short of the glory of God, and are justified freely by his grace through the redemption that came by Jesus Christ.
>
> Romans 3:23

BOOK SIGNING

After careful thought and finally making a decision for the next weaving project, there are times I've been distracted by an unexpected combination of colors, textures, or a new pattern from a weaving magazine. I've stopped and had to rethink my next project.

In life too, sometimes when we're chasing a dream, a better one comes along. That's how I felt as I set up my book display for my first book, *From the Olive Orchard*.

The manager had arranged a space for me; he had set out a table, with my books arranged in displays and several chairs. I covered the table with my hand-woven cloth and added my cards and my pens. Carla, my sister, took a seat next to me. "I have to warn you; we get all kinds of people in this store," the manager shared with me.

Immediately, an older man came over to my table, took a book in his hands, and started thumbing through it. "So are you a Christian?" he asked.

"Yes, I am."

"Well, no one supports Christians anymore. People need to support Christians."

I thought he would be my first sale, but he continued. "Christianity is deteriorating. There's no hope for it. It is at its lowest point ever."

I thought to myself, *Christianity has always been challenged.*

But before I could say anything, he added, "They call me the fighter. I fight for real Christian values."

Just then, some family members found me. I was overwhelmed. They had driven all the way from Sanger, my home, to town. The fighter put down my book and disappeared.

I had just signed their books when an elderly woman stopped at my table. Her body was slightly bent, and she was pushing a walker. She looked at me with thick-framed glasses. I learned that she was a retired teacher, that she had four married children, where they lived, and what they did for a living. She walked away as another person asked me to sign a book she had purchased.

Then the fighter reappeared and picked up my book again. He told me that he was a retired Christian counselor and how he had spent his life working with people of different faiths and beliefs. He added, "The church is in a terrible state today."

As if on cue, the retired teacher reappeared, dragging her walker in front. She continued telling us about her life, her husband, and her family again. "I want to buy your book," she said. "I just have to make sure I have twenty-five dollars left for the taxi. Now, where is my money?" She searched her purse and found an envelope with bills in it. "Oh my, I don't have enough; I don't have enough for the taxi." She panicked.

Carla helped her count her money; it was all there. Then she helped her put the bills back into the envelope and into a front pocket of her purse.

"You don't have to buy the book," I told her several times. "Please keep your money."

"No, no, I really want a copy, and you can sign it." There was a long line at the counter, so my sister volunteered to stand in line for her. She was pleased. A woman stopped by. "Not my kind of book, but good luck with it."

More friends came, bought books, and visited. People I didn't know picked up the book, and several bought copies. One woman saw my table and nervously added, "I go to church. Of course, it's my mother's church. She insisted that I go to her church. She's gone now. I don't have to go to that church, but she wanted me to." Alarm crossed her face. "I can't buy your book. My pastor wrote a book, and I can't buy your book until I buy his first. I have to find it. I have to find it right now." In frenzy, she walked away.

Another shared, "My aunt is a *famous* author. She had her own book signing in Oregon."

The fighter reappeared. He took my book off the display again. "The trouble with the Christian church is all those liberals. They've taken over the church." His apparently memorized dialogue was interrupted by a former special education student of mine. I hadn't seen him for years. He was very grown up. He looked pale, and his skin was flushed from the heat outside. I had him sit next to me. "A book, you have a book? I want to have a copy of your book. You can sign it." He paused and continued, "But I don't have any money."

I assured him that I would work something out later and yes, sign it too.

Then the elderly woman reappeared. My sister took over the conversation. It turned out that they had a common acquaintance in Fresno. The woman was surprised but pleased. She left and found a chair next to a window. Her face was drawn and her eyelids slowly closed.

I saw the fighter approaching out of the corner of my eye. He never made it back to the table. It was time to leave. Carla and David, my husband, helped me to put everything away. I said good-bye to the manager, thanking him. "You were right. You do have lots of different people in your store."

Heaven must be a little like a book signing. You don't know who's going to be coming through the front door.

> Jesus said to them, "I tell you the truth, at the renewal of all things, when the Son of Man sits on his glorious throne, you who have followed me will also sit on the twelve thrones…But many who are first will be last, and many who are last will be first."
>
> Matthew 19:28, 30

> Do not let your hearts be troubled. Trust in God, trust also in me. In my Father's house are many rooms; if it were not so, I would have told you. I am going there to prepare a place for you.
>
> John 14:1–2

CENTERVILLE

Years ago, I taught at Centerville School, a rural kindergarten through eighth grade school just east of Sanger along Highway 180 in California. I knew something about the school because, as a child, my father had taken us on drives throughout the area. His family—my aunts, uncles, and grandparents—had lived nearby before moving into the bigger town of Sanger. There had been a general store, a tavern or two, and a hall where he attended dances with his friends as a young man. Now, these same buildings are worn and dilapidated, barely able to stand on their own. It would only take a breath of wind to knock them over.

This quiet school has been forced into notoriety with the killings of police officers and a suicide. This tragedy took place not too far away, a little farther down Kings Canyon Highway, almost directly across from the Minkler General Store. I remembered the area, the Minkler Store, and also the notorious trailer park nearby. It was a hodgepodge of broken-down trailers and shacks interspaced with skinny eucalyptus trees. It was a picture of poverty left over from the Dust Bowl migration. Several of my students lived there.

One day, one of them told me that his dad was selling firewood and asked if any of the teachers were interested. I said yes. So the next weekend, my husband and I drove out to buy a cord. We picked up my dad in Sanger. At that time, he worked for Fresno County, serving court papers, and often drove into this area. He helped us find the boy's house. The young boy was watching and waved his hand when he recognized me. He called to his dad, who came outside to handle the sale. I looked over at the boy, now standing so quietly near an unsteady, wooden shack. He was watching me too. I walked over to him; he pointed to his house. "That's where I live," he said, looking for my reaction. I peeked inside and saw hardened earth and broken slats for flooring and a young woman sitting silently in a corner, holding a child. He walked over to a cracked hose attached to an outside faucet.

"Here's where I wash up. We don't have any water inside." He paused. "If it's too cold, it freezes. Can't wash."

I didn't know how to answer him, so I just smiled and then said, "That must be difficult." He smiled back at me pleased—pleased to know that I understood. In his own way, he was explaining why he had been coming to school so dirty. In the January cold, he had been arriving with a dirt-streaked face. His blond hair was combed but matted with soot-like dots. His clothes were wrinkled. Even though the students liked him and apparently understood his circumstances, he would sit in the back of the room, keeping away from them. He knew that I had noticed and must have worried that I would say something in front of the class. I never did. Then as the weather became warmer, he came to school with a washed face and body, wearing clean clothes and his hair combed. He smiled at me in pride.

I hadn't thought of this student until I read about the tragedies and the school lockdown. The foundation of his home life had been flawed and broken like a poorly warped loom. His life was like a beginning weaver's project—full of mistakes and problems. In spite of all his difficulties and hurdles, however, God looked beyond his imperfect life and situation. He was a child of God, just like all of us, each one of us valued and loved.

I prayed that he had made it out of poverty and was living a better life. I hoped that the trailer park had changed for the better, because so many good people lived there. So much sorrow had come out of that place, so much unhappiness. Lives lived as twisted and scarred as the eucalyptus trees grasping for life in front of run-down shacks and trailers. God finds us in these desolate and dark places and offers new life with him. Where we live or what we look like doesn't matter. After all, He created us.

> The Lord is close to the brokenhearted and saves those who are crushed in spirit.
>
> Psalm 34:18

> Praise be to the God and Father of our Lord Jesus, the Father of compassion and the God of all comfort.
>
> 2 Corinthians 1:3

FIREPLACE HEARTH

For several months, David had planned to reface our fireplace. It had lost its traditional red brick and mortar crispness. The brick was now chipped in places, it had been painted over several times, and black soot had left deep shadows of gray trails. We picked out some stone and ordered it. Then we waited, and then we waited some more. We waited about a month before we canceled the original order, found another company, and drove to Clovis to pick up the stone ourselves. They loaded it, but we had to unload it. Stone by stone, we finally had our piles off the truck. I kept telling myself that this was great exercise, while David kept an eye out for a possible field crew with a forklift. None appeared. So we finished the job ourselves. Meanwhile, we contacted the mason. This would be a weekend job for him. Thursday, he called and told us that he could begin tomorrow, since Friday would be a furlough day.

So the doorbell rang at seven thirty in the morning, and the work began. He started by tearing out the rounded brick shoulders that continued out of each side of the hearth. They extended across the entire wall. He thought he could save the hearth, but he soon discovered that the hearth brick had been sitting on nothing more than sand. His reaction reminded me of my some of my less-successful weaving projects, where poorly laid foundations had created havoc, frustration, and encumbered the rest of the process. Several times I've had to stop completely and start all over again, wasting time and effort.

"Never pass inspection," he said, shaking his head.

He also found several large ants' nests buried underneath. We had been fighting a trail of ants outside and near the chimney every summer and only guessing at where they might be headed. Now we knew.

As he dug through the mess, he was able to tell us a little something about the person who had laid the hearth. An empty Marlboro carton and cigarette butts meant he was an older man, because that was an old man's brand. "Probably not even a mason. You never know what you might find when you start tearing things apart."

It took two days of preparation before the actual stone could be attached. After the mess with the hearth, the brick had to be stripped of paint, the hearth rebuilt, and the measurements calculated. He pointed out that top of the fireplace was not level. From where I stood, I could see the slight slope. Another black mark for the mystery mason. In the middle of all this prep, there were interruptions. Several times he had to stop, get into his pickup, drive to a dealer, and purchase unanticipated supplies.

Then on Sunday, after two long days of preparation, he started laying the new stone. By Sunday afternoon, everything was done, except for the mantle and some finishing work. Though it may take more than another weekend day, it already looked amazing. It had been worth all the preparation. The foundation was set. The hearth was secure and the mantle level.

The thought occurred to me, *what do we use for a foundation for our lives?* Do we build our lives on false securities and preconceptions, on sands that shift and move? Do we take the time to do it right, build our faith? Living a Christ-based life doesn't guarantee a life without crisis or difficulties, but when troubles do appear, the foundation is already level. It will support us. No surprises. And it is a foundation that will pass any inspection.

> Therefore everyone who hears these words of mine and puts them into practice is like a wise man who built his house on the rock. The rain came down, the streams rose, and the winds blew and beat against that house; yet it did not fall, because it had its foundation on the rock. But everyone who hears these words of mine and does not put them into practice is like a foolish man who built his house on sand. The rain came down, the streams rose, and the winds blew and beat against that house, and it fell with a great crash.
>
> Matthew 7:24–27

WISHING WISHES INTO PRAYER

My class always looked forward to astronomy lessons. So as they eagerly opened their science books to the section on stars, I went to the laptop and logged onto the Internet. My plan was to show a show clip from a science program for elementary children. However, we were quickly sidetracked, or what is called a "teachable moment."

"I saw falling stars," Jerome shared. "Last night. It was like rockets. Lots of them in the dark. Falling all over the place."

"Those were meteors hitting the earth's atmosphere," Ethan stated. "Not stars."

I added,"Yes, Ethan, you're probably right, but they certainly can look like shooting stars."

Melody raised her hand and asked Jerome, "What did you wish for?"

Jerome seemed perplexed.

"When you see a shooting star, you get to make a wish," she added.

Christina added, "But you can't tell the wish, 'cause it won't come true."

"You get to make wishes?" Jerome asked, his eyes wide.

"That's the tradition. If you see a shooting star, you can make a wish," I said.

"I'm making some wishes tonight for sure," Jerome said. By the look on his face, I could tell he had some big wishes swirling around inside his head.

The others began a chorus of their own on the topic of wishes.

"Let's take turns," I said. Hands flew into the air. So after a brief but animated discussion, I gave them a writing assignment: "You may choose one wish. However, there are some rules. Your wish has to be something that can't be bought in a store and, your wish can't be for more wishes."

"Aw," Jerome said. "I can't wish for more wishes?"

"No. That's the rule," I answered.

They eagerly worked on the topic, and all I could hear was the sound of pencils scratching over paper. When school was over for the day, I put aside the other piles of papers on my desk and read their responses, taking the time to enjoy and appreciate their words.

It was the same with Bible reading and study. The demands of the day never ceased, so I learned to create my own space and time for God's Word. Finding the time was renewing and refreshing, just as the children's words.

"I would like more time with my dad. I never get any time with him because he goes to bed at three and works around the clock." Another student: "I don't know my dad. I would like to meet him and say hi."

"I would wish for a better job for my mom. My mom could work hard and get a better house."

"I wish for my mom to come back and never be sick again."

"I wish for my mom to be out of jail. We could talk."

"I would wish for my parents to stop getting in arguments and thinking of getting divorced. I wish for my parents to stop getting mad because of simple things."

Another: "I wish they weren't going to court."

"I wish for no drugs, because my dad uses some, and he gets meaner every time he uses them. Sometimes he's nice, sometimes he's not."

"I would do better in school."

"I would like a friend."

"I wouldn't make a wish. I like my life the way it is."

"I would like more time to think. I need more time to think about things like wishes."

"I can't wish for one thing. I've got lots of wishes. I want a new house, a skateboard, some computer games, and a computer, a credit card for the mini-mart…and a mustang convertible for my grandpa."

Wishes can be a good thing. They can pave the way for open communication between us and God. They can evolve into the beginnings of prayer, which is the groundwork of building a real relationship with Christ. As I sit upon my loom bench weaving, I take time talk to God through my prayers and know he is listening. God hears our prayers anytime, during the day at school, at our jobs or at home. He hears them during the night as we sleep, or watching and wishing upon shooting stars. God listens when we make the time and effort to talk to him and sometimes he may answer by giving us the wishes of our hearts.

> Therefore I tell you, whatever you ask for in prayer, believe that you have received it, and it will be yours.
>
> Mark 11:24

> Whatever you ask in my name, this I will do, that the Father may be glorified in the Son.
>
> John 14:13

THE RAT

We were sitting around a table waiting for the teacher in-service to begin. The principal made one last call on her cell phone to check in with the school's secretary. "A rat?" she asked into the phone. "It wasn't a mouse? He brought a dead rat to school?" Expectant silence lingered over our table as we waited while she listened for an answer.

When the phone conversation ended, she repeated what she had just heard. "Jorge brought a dead rat and put it in one of the girl's backpacks."

Of course, Jorge was one of my students. It never failed! Something always happened when I had a substitute. However, a dead rat had to be given the top honors.

"He was mad at his friend Miguel." Miguel had just returned to school after a suspension and had made a commitment to stay away from students who might be a bad influence on him. Jorge was one of those students. He was angry because his once best friend was ignoring him. So on his way to school that day, he had found a dead rat in the street and decided to carry it to school. When he arrived, he waited until the hall monitor wasn't looking, unzipped what he thought was Miguel's backpack, and dumped the rat inside. It turned out that it wasn't Miguel's backpack at all. Instead, he'd placed the rat in Maria's backpack. Maria was one of those children who somehow managed to balance a traditional Mexican way of life at home with the culture of an American school during the day. She was responsible, earned good grades, and learned English at breathtaking speed. After school, she helped with the younger children while her parents worked long hours in the fields. She certainly hadn't expected to find a dead rat among her carefully organized homework and papers.

I spoke with Jorge the next day. "I was mad," he told me. "I didn't know it was her backpack. I didn't do it on purpose. I was just mad at Miguel. He was my friend, and now he won't hang with me anymore." His voice revealed more hurt over the rejection by his friend rather than the anger I had expected. I let him talk it out.

"It's okay to feel the way you do," I told him, "but hurting someone else doesn't make the hurt go away. It doesn't change things. You just pass the hurt on to someone else."

Rejection can cut deeply. How do we handle the rejection that comes from the world, from those we love or those we expect to love us? Jorge's answer was revenge. He was going to get back at the world, and never mind who got hurt. Often, our first impulse is to react in the same way. That's when we need to look to Christ and remind ourselves that he knew rejection and paid the ultimate price with his life. He took that undeserved pain and suffering and made good with it. He turned it into our salvation. That's good news that fits in anyone's backpack.

But he was pierced for our transgressions, he was crushed for our iniquities; the punishment that brought us peace was upon him, and by his wounds we are healed.

Isaiah 53:5

Therefore, rid yourselves of all malice and deceit, hypocrisy, envy, and slander of every kind. Like newborn babies, crave pure spiritual milk, so that by it you may grow up in your salvation, now that you have tasted that the Lord is good.

1 Peter 2:1–2

A GROWN-UP RAT

One morning as I was walking out of the office just before school began, one of our instructional assistants stopped me. He wanted to show me a picture he had captured on his cell phone the night before. I saw a large commercial truck engulfed in flames and watched as it blew up. "That's what happened in my neighborhood last night."

He explained that the owner of the truck had dismissed an employee over unauthorized, long-distance phone calls. The owner hadn't recognized some of the numbers listed on his phone bill, so he called some of the numbers to find out who had made the calls. He was given the name of one of his employees. However, when questioned, the employee denied ever making the calls. When the employee was faced with the names of the people who verified he had called them, he became angry at his boss. The boss had no right to call those people. The owner had no choice but to fire him. Then the former employee vowed to get back at him.

That same night the owner's truck caught on fire and was destroyed. One of the neighbors managed to move his van to safety as the truck exploded; another car was destroyed in the inferno that followed. Windows cracked and exploded while children slept in their beds.

It was a miracle that no one was hurt or killed. The man had had his revenge even though it meant destroying property, putting innocent people in harm's way, and finding himself arrested and in jail. Never mind who was hurt—his boss would suffer. He had had his payback.

Thinking over this incident, I felt this could be a "grown-up" version of "The Rat" story. Here was a man who blamed his boss for the problems that he had made for himself. When his actions were exposed and he was shown that he was in the wrong, his reaction was retribution. "You can't tell me what to do. You can't fire me." It didn't matter who he hurt or how much damage he caused.

It is so much easier and feels a lot better to blame someone else for our shortcomings, faults, and mistakes. I know. I feel that way when the warped threads continue to break for no apparent reason or I haven't ordered enough yarn to finish a towel. I want to take out my frustration on someone else. When we make those big blunders, embarrass ourselves, or make the wrong choices, do we take our lumps and move forward? Do we get stuck in a quagmire of anger or hatred? Do we rebuild or do we destroy?

> A fool gives full vent to his anger, but a wise man keeps himself under control.
>
> Proverbs 29:11

WILDFLOWERS

I took my fifth graders on a field trip to SCICON, our county's outdoor education camp. In our district, all fifth graders are invited to spend one day at SCICON to prepare them for a week-long stay in the sixth grade. We couldn't have selected a better day. The sun was shining brightly, but the air was cool and fresh. We boarded the traditional yellow bus and left school around nine o'clock in the morning. After a forty-minute ride, we finally arrived at camp, parking in the designated lot for buses, where we were met by two staff members who gave us the rules for SCICON. After all, this was still school and all schools have rules.

The children tumbled off the bus, and after a quick "exploring-the-bathroom" break, they lined up into two rows with a partner. Each line had a camp teacher in the lead. The one standing in front of my group suddenly smiled as she looked over the line of students. With a sparkle in her eye, she decided this would be a great day for an adventure. She winked at me. "I think we should take them on a hike to quartz mine. Usually, we only take sixth graders, but this looks like a good group."

"They are," I answered her.

"Let's go," she said, "but first, the cabins."

So we walked over the Hold Your Breath Bridge and boogied our way over to the cabins, a mandatory stop before hitting the trail. The children peered inside the cabins, which were similar to the ones that they would stay in next year. They saw rustic bunk beds with sleeping bags and pillows neatly flattened over single mattresses. Luggage and personal items were stashed away. A well-used fireplace stood on one end of the room. Walls were plain. Bathrooms and showers were in another building. It wasn't quite like home, but I could tell most of them were up for the challenge.

After leaving the cabins, we followed the path as it edged along a fast-flowing stream to our left, listening to bird chatter and snapping sounds in the brush off the path. We took turns gently holding a confused salamander. When released, it seemed to shake his head at us in disbelief before disappearing back into the damp grasses and slushy mud.

Our trail began to turn away from the stream and into meadows. Dots of individual wildflowers met us. Our guide pointed out a fiddleneck with its heavy stem, a buttercup, and the popcorn flower. The class giggled at the thought that a flower could be called "popcorn." "Watch out for the shooting star," she challenged them. "I saw some around here."

One of the children saw them first: a group of five tiny beings growing by the edge of the path, so fragile. The children formed a circle around the delicate flowers and were careful not to get too close. Silently, they marveled at the sight of the yellow flower faces stretching toward the sun while their blue-purple petals streamed off in the opposite direction.

We turned into a larger meadow and were greeted by a spray of yellow colors swaying in the middle of a vast expanse of spring grasses. I stopped. The scene before me was God's hand-woven tapestry. The wild-flowers swayed in unison as if orchestrated by the gentle wind blowing around us. Each one was individually rooted to its place, never knowing the beauty that they created for my eyes, for our eyes. If only they could have seen their part of the glory in this setting, their toil in the sun might have been lightened.

The children had a great time digging for crystals in the makeshift mine. With sticks and shovels, they dug into the crystal-rich earth, selecting one, and only one, to take home. Those who lost interest explored the edges of the creek nearby or the rim of the grassland, watching for unknown critters. They had been told to stay on the path to avoid ticks lurking in the grass and rattlesnake holes.

Too soon, it was time to leave our prospecting. With disappointing murmurs and jean-cleaned hands, they lined up in single file. We hiked the same trail back, passing the same field of wildflowers, each one remarkable, but the dazzle was gone. The fleeting spectrum of light had shifted; the sun's rays were subdued and restrained. The moment had passed. But then my eyes shifted to the line of quietly walking students ahead of me. As their feet bounced up and down the trail, raising a low fog of dust with their shoes and doing their best to avoid all the ruts and holes, the tops of their heads became a wave of color. Before me was a blending of beiges, golden browns, and chocolate shades and, mixed in the middle, a splat of red. They were not unlike the wildflowers in the field, each one struggling for a place in the sun but coming together in a special moment to create a work of art I knew that with the Lord's hand, each child would find a perfect spot in this world—living and growing together as part of the Lord's design.

We are like the wildflowers in the field, struggling with the day-to-day worries of life, trying to find and hold onto our place in the sun, in the world, not realizing how beautiful we are to the Lord. The Word of God helps us to plant our feet on good soil where we can grow together in God's Word, becoming a part of his masterpiece of humanity. We are woven into his cloth.

> All men are like grass, and all their glory is like the flowers of the field. The grass withers and the flowers fall because the breath of the Lord blows on them. Surely the people are the grass. The grass withers and the flowers fall, but the word of our God stands forever.
>
> Isaiah 40:6–9

WHOSE FAULT IS IT?

I sat next to my friend Susan, a professor at a local college. We were waiting in the doctor's office for an appointment with her doctor. She had been diagnosed with cancer and had undergone surgery four years ago. This was a follow-up appointment, and she was waiting to hear the results of her blood tests. She had asked me to come along for the dreaded follow-up.

Most of the seats in the room were taken. People of various ages, body types, and ethnic backgrounds filled the room. Some of the patients knew each other and nodded in acknowledgment.

"This is a heck of a place to see you," one of the men said to the man sitting next to me.

"Ain't it though," he answered.

Most sat silently, flipping through magazines and checking watches out of nervousness. The waiting room was quiet, heads bent down as a woman left in tears, an older woman by her side.

I couldn't tell from outward appearances which of those waiting had been diagnosed with cancer. Only the doctor with his charts and lab test results could separate the patients from the visitors.

So I asked those same questions. Why does cancer touch some and not others? Why do wonderful people have to go through this? Whose fault was it? Was it caused by the wrong combination of genes passed on by a parent or grandparent? Was it diet? Surely diet must have something to do with it. Smoking was a culprit for sure, but what about alcohol and drug addictions? Perhaps there had been too much partying or maybe not enough. All that stress was unhealthy too. Pollution, the air we breathe, or the nitrates in the drinking water were all possibilities. Not one of us in that room, asking those questions, knew for sure. No one had the answers.

If only we could be cured of our diseases, just like Jesus cured the blind man in John 9. However, we know that it doesn't always end that way. We can be a testimony to Christ during these times of trial. We can pray. Our families and friends can pray.

Susan and I walked out of the office with encouraging news. Her blood tests were normal. As we climbed into the car, one of Susan's students called out, "Ms. G, how are you doing?"

"Just fine." She smiled.

"Well, I want you to know I've been praying for you."

"Thank you. It helps more than you know."

> As he walked along, he saw a man blind from birth. His disciples asked him, "Rabbi, who sinned, this man or his parents, that he was born blind?"
>
> "Neither this man nor his parents sinned," said Jesus, "but this happened so that the work of God might be displayed in his life.
>
> John 9:1–3

SURVIVORS

The phone rang. "Hello," I answered.

"This is Christina." It was a child's voice. "You were my teacher?"

"Yes, Christina. This is a surprise."

She added, "We're staying in a motel room, my brother and sisters. My mom too. We were bored and found two books in the room. One was a Bible, but we didn't understand it, so we found a phone book and were looking up names and found your number. So I called to talk to you." Silence. "What are you doing?"

"Well, Christina, I was working in the yard." I paused. "Why are you in a motel room?"

"We were in the shelter and didn't have any place to go. We're moving into a house tomorrow." I knew this wasn't the first time the family had ended up in the shelter and it wouldn't be the last time.

I asked her, "Do you need some food?" She gave me her new address and the next day, David and I loaded up the truck with food and toiletries and delivered them to the family. We were greeted with smiles and laughter by the children. Their mother was delighted and thanked us in Spanish numerous times as we unloaded our truck. "Christina, you call me if you ever need food."

Since her house was in another school district, I knew the children wouldn't be returning to my school. So I contacted the school's community liaison, who knew the family dynamics, and shared this incident with him.

"The father is an alcoholic—in and out of the picture. Like so many other families, I can't get them help because they don't have papers, that is, except for the baby who was born here."

He agreed to keep me informed. I told him we'd get some things for Thanksgiving but didn't want others to know. Early on in my teaching career, I learned that once word got around that I had helped out a student or family, others lined up for help whether they needed help or not. Too many hurt feelings.

About a year later, I received a call from Christina, now in middle school. "Mrs. Bezayiff, we're moving into an apartment. It's a better place."

"Wonderful," I said.

"But we need four hundred dollars to move in. My mother said she will pay you back in two weeks. She gets a check in two weeks."

"Christina, I'm sorry but I don't have four hundred dollars."

"You don't?" she asked, surprised. There was some talking in the background. "How about some of your friends? Do some of your friends have four hundred dollars? We can pay it back."

"No," I answered. "I don't know anyone who has that kind of money. I can bring over some food, but not money." So we brought one last load of basic food supplies. As we left, I saw their father rummaging through the boxes of food, the children and mother off to the side.

The liaison also shared with me, "This is the time of the year that their father leaves for Mexico for a few weeks, leaving the family to take care of themselves. The children want to stay in school and don't want to leave." This was when the borders between the countries were still open.

A couple of years later I saw Christina and asked her how she was doing. The family was living in a rented room in someone's house. "We're okay. I know where to get help when we need it." She smiled with confidence.

"I'll be praying for you, Christina." As much as I wanted a better life for Christina and her family, I realized I couldn't fix her lifestyle with money, time, or my limited supply of energy. I would continue to support the shelters and food banks in my community, but ultimately, they were in the Lord's hands. He would be the strength as they reworked the warp, the foundations of their lives.

As she walked away, I knew she would endure. She knew where to find food, shelter, and protection for her family; she had learned the system. She was a survivor.

Christians are survivors too. We are the ultimate survivors because we know that Jesus loved us so much that he endured death on the cross to free us from our sins. Even as we face difficulties and obstacles, some that we bring upon ourselves, or those imposed upon us from others, we know the system. It is the Word of God found in the Bible. It works. Just open the Bible and see where it leads you.

> The unfolding of your words give light, it gives understanding to the simple.
>
> Psalm 119:130

FLOODING, A WEDDING, AND AN IRIS IN BLOOM

The week before Christmas, we drove to Los Angeles for a family wedding. It was a tense and anxious trip. The rain had been relentless, each mile a challenge. The windshield wipers worked on overdrive. Interstate-5 through the Grapevine pass had remained open in spite of the freezing temperatures and thick rain, its closure our greatest worry.

Our first stop was Burbank, where we left my sister, who would drive Uncle Peter and Aunt Lee to their grandson's wedding. We found a hotel and connected with cousins Bob and Sue, who were also going to the wedding. Exhausted from the drive, no one looked forward to driving in the heavy rain and dark skies forming outside our window. It was almost five o'clock, but it felt like midnight. The wedding was at the Cathedral of Our Lady of the Angels in downtown LA. Usually this wouldn't have been a problem, but now, in the clouded, rain-soaked sky, it would be difficult to find, even with written directions and our navigation system, which almost had a meltdown. Highways 101, 110, 10, Interstate-5, connections to San Bernardino, and Pomona

60 all seemed to converge near our Temple Street exit. We blindly found the exit and parked in an underground parking garage adjacent to the church. At least we would be free from the storm during the ceremony. As we entered the church, its warmth and peace washed over us and tempered our weariness. The monsignor performed a wedding filled with Christian love. He pointed out that the light from inside the cathedral was emanating out through the alabaster cross in the ceiling and shining as a witness to the outside dark rainy world. I was reminded of Matthew 5:16: "In the same way, let your light shine before men, that they may see your good deeds and praise your Father in heaven." As we joined in prayer for the new couple, many of us added silent prayers for safe travel. With the ceremony over, the reception began and we experienced a wonderful celebration.

The next day we drove to the airport to pick up our son, who had flown in for Christmas. On the way, we avoided several accidents as speeding cars hydroplaned across freeways. We were nearly hit by a loose tire as a car skidded across the highway in front of us and crashed against the cement barrier to our left. We pulled over to call 911. They were already on overload, even though it was only eight o'clock. Tow trucks and police cars were parked on off ramps and turnoffs. We were relieved to pick up Nate and be on our way home. LA traffic is never for the faint of heart, but this time it had been horrific, even by LA standards.

With relief, we drove into our driveway, but the relief was short lived. Our orchard was flooded. Tulare County had been declared a disaster area. So much rain!

Then we saw it. It was an iris in full bloom. An iris in bloom is a singular thing of beauty. An iris in bloom in December is an extraordinary event. It stood straight and perfectly formed in a puddle of water just outside our kitchen window. Its sun-yellow petals formed a pedestal for the tower of pure white bloom innocent of winter's presence, the freezing cold, and the four inches of rain dropped in less than two days. Within a day we found another one, the same colors, but with all three blossoms in bloom. Then a week later, just to make sure we hadn't missed the point, one more bloomed. This bloom was painted in purples with white streaks. It grew in Catherine's garden, a garden David had planted for me after my mother's death. He had collected bricks and plants from her house and wove them into a pathway of herbs and irises. David weaves our garden as I weave cloth from the loom.

Was it a message, a sign, a blessing, or merely an oddity of nature? Whatever its purpose, it stood as a promise of spring and optimism in the midst of a cold and flooded valley.

Christ allows the storms to rage so that we might turn to him, listening for his message. He also offers a promise of spring, of renewed life and rebuilding even from life's angry rainstorms. We may have to live through some bad times, but his promise is as real as an iris blooming in winter.

> He says to the snow, "Fall on the earth," and to the rain shower, "Be a mighty downpour." So that all men he has made may know his work, he stops every man from his labor.
>
> Job 37:6–7

MUSIC TO OUR EARS

I've often heard there's a special place in heaven for teachers. If that is true, then the first chair definitely belongs to elementary school music teachers.

The annual spring concert for the instrumental strings students was held at the junior high school auditorium. The concert was scheduled for seven, but I arrived early to offer support and encouragement to my students. Already, an intent but nervous group had formed under their school poster. They were practicing at preparation. Their strings were fixed taut, loosened, then tightened; the process repeated again and again. The disorganized notes mixed in well with the clamor of small children, complaining babies, and adult conversation—most taking place on cell phones. The would-be performers listened carefully for a matching note as the music teachers traveled from one group to another. Then the students worked their strings and bows, and somehow managed to tune those instruments to some magical key that hung over the entire room, forming a pleasing weaving of musical notes.

The youthful musicians took their ordered places in front of the stage. Many of the girls wore simple skirts and trendy matching tops—big, bright bows sat on curled hair or pulled ponytails. Some of the boys wore traditional white shirts and black pants. One or two wore a tie. Heads of hair had been combed and parted, while others stood wild and independent.

The performers quieted even as their eyes nervously probed the audience, searching for family and friends. Before them, the audience sat in rows of quietly squeaking folding chairs. Then the conductor began the program. Hands uplifted, each musician watching for the signal; they began traditional rhythms and scales of beginning musicians. The notes didn't all come together in perfect unison, but the intent was indisputable. They worked through their list of music, each piece decidedly more complicated than the last. Music of Beethoven and Bach filled the auditorium-turned-symphony-hall. Even as the more advanced students shared their pieces, it was amazing to me that they had learned so much in such a short time. These were the children of field workers, single parents, and working poor.

A few months before, during their first lesson, the teacher had directed them to open their music cases and said, "This is a violin, these are strings, and this is a bow. Place the instrument like this, and move the bow back and forth. This is how you start." The foundation had been laid.

Yes, this is how it starts. It starts with people who have made music their life's work and have found themselves sharing that gift with young children. The tedious repetition of weekly instructions and misplaced notes would defeat most professionals, but not all. Those who stay with it know that the reward is great. The reward is knowing that the geniuses of the world's music have found a presence in our schools, tucked among the orchards and fields of our community and in our churches. The love of music continues with the next generation.

Music is another way to praise and thank God for all our blessings. I sing to the Lord, thanking him for these untiring workers who share their love of music with children.

> Speak to one another with psalms, hymns and spiritual songs. Sing and make music in your heart to the Lord, always giving thanks to God the Father for everything, in the name of our Lord Jesus Christ.
>
> Ephesians 5:19–20

LAURA INGALLS WILDER:PIONEER WOMAN OF FAITH

It's never too late to begin something new. I realized this while touring the Laura Ingalls Wilder Museum in Mansfield, Missouri. Once inside the museum, the first thing I spotted was Pa's fiddle enclosed in a glass case. Suddenly, Laura's stories and her life became real to me.

Laura Ingalls Wilder was sixty years old when she wrote her first book *Little House in the Big Woods*. After a lifetime of experiences and far from the settings of her stories, she wrote her books from a simple desk at her Rocky Ridge Farm. Her books, describing her life as child growing up in a pioneer family, have been shared with generations of children all over the world. Many of us grew up reading these stories or watching *Little House on the Prairie* on television. The last book she published was *These Happy Golden Years*; however, those golden years were short-lived. She wrote an account of her later life, *The First Four Years*, but never had the heart to publish it. It was finally published after her death.

She called these years her time of sunshine and shadow. There were more shadows than sunshine.

Laura and Almanzo, Laura called him Manley for short, were married in 1885 in DeSmet in Dakota territory. Aside from the birth of their daughter, Rose, the young couple experienced devastation and ruin. First, their barn and haystacks burned to the ground. Because of crop failures, they couldn't pay their debts. They came down with diphtheria, and neither could work for weeks. Laura's mother took care of Rose during this time. Laura recuperated, but Manley had a stroke that left him with a limp for the rest of his life. Life seemed to improve, but then Laura gave birth to a baby boy who died twelve days later from convulsions. The house that Manley had built burned to the ground. They lost everything. Laura managed to save a glass bread plate with these words on the rim: "Give Us This Day Our Daily Bread." She kept the plate for the rest of her life, the words providing a strong foundation and strength for their lives.

Their determination was steadfast, and their faith was strong; they would begin again. They built a two-room shanty, but their crops failed again; this time, they lost their land. They lived with family, tried Florida, but returned to DeSmet. They worked at odd jobs and saved wages. Even though she hated sewing, Laura found a job as a seamstress to earn money. Finally, after seven years of marriage, they saved one hundred dollars— enough to put a down payment on a farm in Missouri in the Ozark Mountains. With their daughter, Rose, they packed up their covered wagon and said good-bye to Ma, Pa, Mary, Carrie, Grace, and friends. It took them forty-five days to travel to Mansfield, Missouri. Once there, Laura thought they had lost the hundred dollars, but it had slipped under the cloth in her writing desk. Finally, they were able to give the bank a down payment. Laura named their home Rocky Ridge Farm. There, they built a house, planted crops, and prospered, making a life for themselves and Rose. Throughout her life, Laura never lost that pioneer spirit of perseverance and faith. The memories of Pa's fiddle helped too—a reminder of better times and happiness.

Throughout her books, she wrote about the values of life. She named them, "courage, self-reliance, independence, integrity, and helpfulness. Cheerfulness and humor were handmaids to courage." People of all faiths and religions identify with these values. That's why her stories are so universal. Her books also remind us of the American pioneer character and the strength to rebuild and begin again in spite of everything. Her life with Manley personifies that unfaltering spirit and of what we are capable of surviving and accomplishing.

> This, then, is how you should pray: "Our Father in heaven, hallowed be your name, your kingdom come, your will be done on earth as it is in heaven. Give us today our daily bread. Forgive us our debts as we also have forgiven our debtors, and lead us not into temptation, but deliver us from the evil one."
>
> Matthew 6:9–13

STEP 2:

Warping Up

Setting the warp and preparing the weft are at the heart of weaving. The quality of the final project is directly dependent on the skill, time, and energy that goes into this step. So too is the desire to seek and study the Word of God at the heart of knowing Christ. Study brings us to a new level of understanding as we dig deeper for meaning in our spiritual lives and a closer union with God. Fellowship with other Christians adds to this strong foundation. If I encounter difficulties or problems with my weaving, I seek out other weavers for assistance or take classes to improve my skills. Christians need fellowship too. We can't go at it alone. Through activities such as Bible study, book discussions, prayer groups, and, of course, worship, we lay the groundwork for the final fabric.

Warp: Yarns Tied from Front to Back

Warping depends on several factors. After deciding upon the finished length of the piece, add an extra amount of length for waste. There is always waste. Yarn that is tied to the loom cannot be woven but can be a fringe for the finished piece.

Then find the number of warp ends per inch. That is, calculate how many individual pieces of yarn cover an inch space.

After calculating the number of warp ends per inch, multiply that number by the length of the finished project. Then multiply this number by the width of the piece. Always buy more yarn than calculated.

Weft: Yarn from Left to Right

Most projects require an equal amount of yarn for the weft. Weft is the single pieces of yarn that are woven in and out of the warping. Weft can be calculated by counting the number of rows of weft (yarn) that are needed to cover one inch. The amount of weft needed is the number of rows per inch times the width of the piece times the length of the pieces. Again, always buy more than calculated.

After the calculations for the weft have been completed, wrap the yarn into balls. String the warp yarns from the balls individually through the reed and then the heddles. Next, gather the individual warp ends at the back of the loom and knot into groups. Secure the knots to the back of the loom. Wind the warp as you work. Then secure the yarn ends in front to the front beam in a similar manner.

ALPACA HERDS
AND FELLOWSHIP

One of the members of the Hand Weaver's Guild arranged for a visit to an alpaca-breeding farm. Most of us had never been on the farm, even though it was less than an hour from town. Before our arrival, the owner separated out a few female alpacas from the herd and placed them into a nearby pen so that we could touch them later. As she began her talk to our standing outside the shearing barn, the alpacas became agitated and started pressing against the bars of the enclosure, endangering themselves. Concerned for their safety, she opened the gate, and they sprinted away, rejoining the herd. Their security was in their herd, but the owner also thought it might have something to do with the recent shearing. They hated shearing, even though they appreciated the absence of fur during the heat.

The owner continued and then answered questions. Several of us standing in the back were clearly distracted by the animals nearby in another enclosure. Playful and curious, they watched us, chewing on grasses from the spring rains. Their faces were covered in soft fur, and they seemed so huggable. They appeared more approachable, unlike their strong-willed llama cousins.

The spinners in the group were especially excited because the alpacas had just been sheared and their fleece was available for sale. Oversized plastic bags filled with alpaca wool sat on makeshift tables, ready for sale. I learned that alpaca fur is very desirable. It has soft, lustrous, silky fibers and is warmer than sheep's wool. Sheep's wool contains lanolin but alpaca fur doesn't, so it doesn't repel water. When the owner finished speaking, the spinners immediately went for the bags.

Though I have always appreciated the skill that goes into spinning, I've never ventured into that realm of fiber art. Weaving is enough of a challenge. Picking out debris, carding, and washing fur in preparation for spinning on a spinning wheel was always a forever task to me. Instead, I walked over to the enclosure to get a better look at the animals staring at me from a safe distance. They obviously felt protected and sheltered in their family groups, especially the younger ones, called crias. They huddled tightly within the group as close as possible to their mothers. Alpacas are passive animals and not aggressive in nature. Away from the herd, they were vulnerable and helpless. They needed protection from the outside world, which included coyotes as well as domesticated and feral cats and dogs. The owners had gone to a great deal of expense building high fences and strong gates for added protection.

Human beings have herds too. We call them families. Generally, they are wonderful and caring, but sometimes, instead of protecting and nurturing, they can be as destructive as outside world forces. When seeking a positive place in this world, a place of light, we can turn to our Christian family. Jesus is the leader, the protector. He does not disappoint. His family is gender blind—without regard to race, color, investment portfolio, parental background, cholesterol level, or credit card debt. The only requirement is that you seek a living spiritual union with God and acknowledge him as your savior.

> We proclaim to you what we have seen and heard, so that you also may have fellowship with us. And our fellowship is with the Father and with his Son, Jesus Christ. We write this to make our joy complete.
>
> 1 John 1:3–4

GRACIE AND
THE ANGELS

I wish that you could have known Gracie. She taught me to appreciate the craziness of the Christmas season. She absolutely loved Christmas. The hustle and bustle, the commotion, the noise, and the commercialism didn't bother her. She thrived on it. The elegant decorations that transformed the malls, Christmas choirs singing carols, and children lining up to visit Santa were all part of the experience. She would order a cup of coffee and maybe a sandwich for lunch and sit at a table nearby Santa's workshop. She'd watch the little ones, some so serious in the anticipation of meeting Santa, while others were crying, reaching for their mothers with outstretched arms. Some were laughing, giggling, even fascinated by Santa, and some trying a tug at his beard.

The packages piled up in the spare bedroom until wrapping day and then transferred to the dining table, where the process would begin. Out came colorful wrapping paper, multi-colored bows, and shiny ribbons. Scotch tape, new scissors, and tags appeared, saved from last year's after-Christmas sales. Several times, I was able to help her with all the wrapping and sorting.

"Who is this for?" I asked, cutting off the price tag.

"Oh, that's for me," she answered a little sheepishly. "I just had to buy a gift for myself. Wrap it and put it under the tree."

In the end, each carefully wrapped package found a place in boxes for mailing or under the tree. She loved having a Christmas tree with all its decorations and lights. She was childlike in her enthusiasm as she decorated the living room with her angels and velvet Santas. Dolls had a special place in her Christmas room. She stopped decorating a tree, however, after her husband died. "It just isn't the same," she would say.

However, even in her later years, she enjoyed and looked forward to Christmas dinner at her home. She would spend days ironing the linen tablecloths and napkins, cleaning china, and polishing silverware. It took hours of shopping and planning, but her meals were as delicious as they were elegantly served.

Gracie was a child of immigrant parents. She grew up in East Los Angeles and at a young age, worked as a servant for wealthy families. They taught her about the possibilities of life, the nice things, and hard work, earning your keep. She had many jobs during her life, one of which was weaving rugs in a mill. There she worked the looms by hand until more modern machinery was purchased, and then pounded the hard cement floors with her calloused feet, organizing the final details for shipping orders. She had a small profit-sharing plan in the company but lost it all when the company closed.

"Never mind," she said. " I have my home. I know how to work. Christ provides." Later, she babysat to earn a few dollars and became a nanny for two little girls. She worked hard but enjoyed life, especially giving to others. She carried the spirit of Christ all year round. She always had a few dollars for fellow workers who needed a loan and was always surprised when repaid. She spent hours making beautiful cloth dolls and stuffed toys for a local hospital. She was constantly contributing to causes and helping those in need.

She fed strangers at her door in spite of our warnings and concern over her safety.

But she would answer simply, "Mother told me to be generous. You never know when you might be entertaining angels."

How about you?

Will you be entertaining angels anytime soon?

> Give, and it will be given to you. A good measure, pressed down, shaken together and running over, will be poured into your lap. For the measurement you use, it will be measured to you.
>
> Luke 6: 38

> You yourselves know that these hands of mine have supplied my own needs and the needs of my companions. In everything I did, I showed you that by this kind of hard work we must help the weak, remembering the words the Lord Jesus himself said: "It is more blessed to give than to receive."
>
> Acts 20:34–35

> Keep on loving each other as brothers. Do not forget to entertain strangers, for by so doing some people have entertained angels without knowing it.
>
> Hebrews 13: 2

THE TOE

We had an unexpected disruption for our New Year. It was an infected toe. About a week before Christmas, the red from David's toe began spreading up his foot. Even he realized it was time to see the doctor. None of us could figure out the cause. It didn't look like a spider bite—maybe bacteria from a cut or rubbing from a new pair of shoes? We left the pharmacy that day with heavy medication, powders and salts, and a tub for soaking. We would be seeing the doctor more than we would get to see our families during the holidays.

David hobbled around quite comfortably, but we wouldn't be going anywhere else. I realized that the time spent around the house was relaxing. After boxing up the Christmas decorations and taking out the tree, I started a list in my head. Teachers always make lists; it's an occupational habit. First, I warped up my loom, now able to work on a project that I had been planning for months. I pulled out a stack of neglected books to read, games came out of the closet, and watching the rainstorms from the windows was engaging. The foothills of the Sierra Nevada Mountains turned from brown to carpet green right before our eyes, and the usually hidden rows of snow-capped, icy-blue mountains appeared in crystal clarity.

I took walks and hiked with our children. A stray dog followed us and then disappeared into one of the orange groves. We noticed the wildlife scurrying around the orchard, a family of quail, a couple skittish jackrabbits and birds pecking at the insects in our sad-looking garden.

I was able to answer e-mails, meet some friends for lunch, and catch up on what was going on in their lives. I cleaned some of those corners that I had been missing and began going through piles of papers and magazines rediscovered in baskets stashed away in closets. The laundry didn't get behind, and the dishwasher was always empty. Almost scary.

David was delighted to have an excuse to watch all the football and basketball games on television. He had his own stack of books and magazines. We watched a couple of debates on television and rented some movies. As nice as it sounds, however, it didn't take too long to know that we both had cabin fever.

Who would ever have guessed that an innocent toe could affect so many people and disrupt so many plans?

Reflecting on a Bible passage, I was reminded that we are all members of the body of Christ. We each have our part. Some of us are the mouth, some are the heart, and some of us are small toes. It really doesn't matter how we fit together, except that when one member is hurting, it affects the whole body. We are all connected through Christ.

> Just as each of us has one body with many members, and these members do not all have the same function, so in Christ we who are many form one body, and each member belongs to all the others.
>
> Romans 12:4–5

TRAVELING THE HIGHWAYS WITH CHILDREN

Our nephew, Andrew, and our niece, Natalie, left their home in the Los Angeles area about 9:30 one Saturday morning. This was no small task. Their car had been packed with toys, snacks, and other necessities for a car trip with four young children. Amazingly, the family had been fed, dressed, and buckled into car seats without any serious delays—an organizational feat to say the least.

We had invited them for a family celebration at our home. They made arrangements to leave early that morning so they could spend most of the day with us, but things did not work out as planned.

Morning turned into early afternoon, and early afternoon turned into late afternoon. The other family members began arriving, but not this young family. *Something's up*, I thought and said a quiet prayer. Then Andrew's parents arrived and told us that they had spoken with them on their cell phone. Their car was parked on a shoulder of Highway 99 just south of Bakersfield. The family was waiting in the intense 95-degree heat for a roadside service to come and help with a flat tire.

This was not the first delay. They had been stalled on Interstate-5 over the Grapevine for a couple of hours— first, because of a truck accident (it had turned over on its side), and then because of another grass fire near the end of the ridge. Finally, they turned off the highway but got off on the wrong exit, so it took them a few more tries to find out place.

We were all relieved when they finally arrived. Hannah, Jakob, Sophia, and Mikayla bounced out of the car, as only children can do, with hugs and smiles. Their mom and dad obviously needed something cold to drink and a little quiet time to recoup their energy. The rest of the day went fairly well. They each had a turn on the loom. Jakob did manage to get caught in the ropes of the pool sweep, but my brother was watching nearby and jumped in after him, pulling him out quickly. He was back into the pool in no time. Soon, it was time to shower and dress them for the long ride home.

About fifteen minutes after they left, I found their swimsuits in the laundry room. I didn't have the heart to call them on the cell phone and tell them about the suits. David would mail them on Monday. They called us once they had gotten through the Grapevine and were almost home, exhausted and tired for sure. The next day would also be a big day with lots of excitement. They were meeting at their cousins,' Luke and Alex's, home for Luke's sixth birthday party. Hopefully the day would be less complicated.

All of us make plans and preparations throughout our lives. We try to map out and think ahead, turning over in our minds the myriad of possibilities we may encounter. However, no matter how hard we try to predict outcomes, in the end, we have to depend on blind trust that everything will turn out as it should, which includes traveling the highways with children.

Trust is based on faith. Christian faith comes from knowing Jesus. Knowing Jesus, we understand that we may get where we want, but He will decide how we get there and when.

> Now faith is being sure of what we hope for and certain of what we do not see.
>
> Hebrews 11:1

TRUSTING OUR FOUNDATIONS

I heard this story from David's uncle just after I married into the family. He told of a father who wanted to teach his young child a lesson about life. The first thing he did was place the child on the top of a kitchen table and tell him to jump. The child hesitated but knew his father was close by and would catch him. The child jumped off the edge of the table, but instead of being caught by his father's arms, his father let him fall to the floor. He hurt his legs and cried from the pain. "So let that be a lesson to you," his father scolded him. "Trust no one in this life."

I have thought about this story. It seems that we are quickly becoming a nation that does not trust. Gas prices soared while gas companies' profits rocketed to the highest levels ever. We now find that our ability to pay these prices to fill our gas tanks is competing with our food and energy budgets. A full tank of gas, or food for the family? Then there are those who have lost or on the verge of losing homes and businesses—first, because of the climbing variable interest rates and plummeting home prices, and now, mortgage foreclosures. Too often potential buyers were told by lending institutions, who knew better, that it didn't matter if a homeowner didn't have a down payment or the income to pay exorbitant mortgage payments if the rates began climbing. Many jobs that we thought were secure have disappeared. Those who have invested their money in the stock market cannot depend on those investments for their children's college or retirement. Added to all this was the gulf oil spill that added to the misery of lost incomes and destruction of the gulf waters and wildlife.

A small business owner with a shop on Main Street told me her story. She had decided to open her own place a few years ago. When she went to buy a loan, she was given one with a variable interest rate. She was a little worried about the loan; something about it kept nagging at her. So she decided to take out a second mortgage on her home instead and paid off the original loan. She told me later that if she hadn't done that, she would have lost both her business and her home.

In addition to the economic difficulties, friends shared with me the painful break up of marriages. How do they ever trust again when the people who promised to love them for the rest of their lives toss aside that love and commitment? How do we trust each other when we have been so hurt?

How do we trust when our foundations have fallen apart?

Jesus is the answer, of course. When we seriously study his Word, we know in our hearts that he does not disappoint. We can trust him to be a support for us when everything around us crumbles and breaks apart.

He will not forget us. His loving arms are there to catch us as we fall and then lift us up.

> Trust in the Lord with all your heart and lean not on your own understanding; in all ways acknowledge him, and he will make your paths straight.
>
> Proverbs 3:5–6

BEE BOXES

I was busy in the kitchen with my list of Saturday tasks when David called to me. "You have to come with me. Forget what you're doing. I want you to see this." Intrigued and more than a little willing to put aside the household chores, I followed him and climbed into the truck. We drove out onto Highway 65 and turned off on a country road outside Visalia. He parked in front of an open gate that led down a rutted, dirt road. On either side stood several dilapidated mobile homes that had been converted into living quarters. Stacks of discarded items in various stages of decay and ruin were scattered everywhere. *Was someone sleeping under a torn tent in the back?*

"Look, see the bee boxes back in the corner." I followed his gaze and saw a disorganized pile of the boxes in the back of the property. "Are you going to raise bees?" I questioned. Ignoring me, David got out of the truck, and immediately, four huge dogs barreled out of nowhere. "Get back in the truck," I called after him. The dogs stopped in their tracks, sniffed him but didn't bother him. David called out to someone in one of the houses, but no one appeared. Thank goodness!

Finally, back in the truck, he answered my questioning stare. "I was driving around and spotted those bee boxes. I thought I'd fill them with dirt and plant tulip bulbs for spring."

Just then another pickup truck pulled up alongside of us. The driver was also in the bee business but didn't live on the property. He didn't know if the bee boxes on the property were for sale. He explained that the people living there were not the ones we wanted to do business with. "They're a tough bunch," he told us. We were quickly on our way.

David would not be deterred. A couple of weeks later, a student at the college drove into our driveway with a pickup bed full of boxes. His family ran a small business selling honey that they collected from hives inside of bee boxes. They were more than happy to deliver the broken, bottomless, and cracked boxes to our home.

So the next weekend David spent the afternoon placing bee boxes all over our yard. He filled them with soil, planted 350 bulbs, and we waited for the promise of spring.

Just as David was able to see the possibility of something new growing in unwanted, cracked, and broken boxes, Christ finds us in all stages of our lives. He finds us and recycles his own beauty within us. He fills his old boxes with new life and eternal splendor. We don't even have to wait for spring.

> And this is the testimony: God has given us eternal life, and this life is in his Son. He who has the Son in his life; he who does not have the Son of God does not have life.
>
> 1 John 5:11–12

EARTHQUAKE

We drove south for Sophia and Mikayla's fourth birthday. The twins' party took place at their grandparents' house, David's sister and brother-in-law. Shortly after we arrived all six of their grandchildren came running into their house and lavished us with hugs and kisses. They were dressed in birthday party splendor. The twin girls were in matching, pink-inspired outfits, except for the shoes. They made sure that their shoes never matched.

Their excitement was contagious and their anticipation infectious. The girls hardly touched their food but waited patiently to open their presents.

After many *ahs*, the presents all opened, and the candles on the birthday cake blown out, it was time for them to pack up and head for home.

We had breakfast with all of them the next day, but on Tuesday, David's sister, Patty, suggested that we take the time to shop for yardage in the garment district of downtown Los Angeles. I had never been there and was looking forward to the adventure. David followed in our truck so I could call him on the cell phone if we became separated.

We enjoyed wandering from shop to shop, poking among the bolts of yardage that covered the walls from floor to ceiling. Rolls of yardage stood on their ends outside the entryways like colorful people waiting for a parade. Men with carts of yardage and other goods pushed past them, not unlike the Egyptian merchants we had seen in Cairo. While inside one of the stores, we heard a loud *boom*. I immediately thought of an airplane hitting the ground. Then the walls began to shake.

I looked at Patty, and we said, "Earthquake," simultaneously. We turned around and headed for the street. Outside people were everywhere, most on cell phones trying to get information. The cell phones went dead.

After a hectic few minutes, people went back into the stores. Movement returned to streets, and selling and buying resumed. We decided the best thing to do was have lunch and then leave for home. Once in our cars, we thought David had followed us out of the parking lot, but we realized we had lost him. I tried the cell phone, but the service had been disconnected. We doubled back but couldn't find him. So we decided that the best thing was to continue on and wait for him at the restaurant.

I finally got a voicemail from David: "Pick up your phone. I don't know where you are." There was definitely an edge to his voice. Just then, Bill got through to Patty using a land phone. It had been an earthquake in the Chino Hills area, not too far from their home but not in downtown Los Angeles. Patty asked Bill to call David and give him directions. My cell phone finally was able to connect to his too.

We stood on the corner, and after a long, apprehensive time, we spotted David's truck. It wasn't too long after we were enjoying famous French dip sandwiches and ice-cold drinks.

David told us what had happened. He had followed us out of the parking lot but thought we had turned right. When he came around the block again, a police car forced him to turn in the opposite direction and follow behind a bus full of people. Suddenly, a man jumped on the bumper of the bus in front of him while other protesters, with their signs and banners, walked alongside his truck. He had involuntarily joined a protest march by the Community Action Network supporting the homeless. For a brief moment, he thought he should take out his guitar and sing a chorus of "We Shall Overcome." Finally, the huge parade of demonstrators arrived at the Union Rescue Mission, and he was able to drive away. By that time, he had connected with Bill by phone and quickly found us.

How many times do we find ourselves in apprehensive situations or misled by people with good and sometimes not-so-good intentions? Do we find enough strength to trust in the Lord? Do we rely on the Lord to get us moving in the right direction?

> The Lord watches over you—the Lord is your shade at your right hand; the sun will not harm you by day nor the moon by night. The Lord will keep you from all harm—he will watch over your life; the Lord will watch over your coming and going both now and forevermore.
>
> Psalm 121:5–8

BUTTERFLY HOUSE

The first five years of my life, we lived on the family ranch. The house was a single-level wooden building. A screen porch enclosed the front of the house. In the back was a tank house with a stairway that ended in a forbidden darkness at the top. I never ventured into the chicken coop either; a nasty old rooster liked to chase after me. Rows of grape vines were twisted with wire and secured on thick posts. The posts were splintered and rough. Standing next to them, I would try to catch a glimpse of my dad working in the furrows.

Sometimes, my mother would take out the Taylor tot, a heavy metal stroller. The baby, Jimmy, would go in front. As she secured Carla behind him in the same seat, I would show him how to move the beads on the wire in the tray in front of him. He'd bang on them, and I'd give up. A diaper bag fit behind Carla or in the curved place in the back where the handles connected to the body of the stroller. I'd walk along next to her. If I got too tired, she would move the bag, and I could stand over the tops of the metal that covered the wheels.

We would walk down Indianola Avenue and enjoy the spring air. Mom would stop so I could pick wild-flowers. My hand bouquets became droopy and lifeless. So I'd drop them and start all over again until I tired of playing a game I couldn't win. Once, we ended up at Uncle Joe and Aunt Emma's ranch. As we walked down the dirt-packed driveway, Uncle Joe waved to us. Aunt Emma brought out chairs. Mom helped Carla out of the Taylor tot. Then she laid Jimmy on a quilted blanket on the lawn.

Quickly, we became bored. Looking around the ranch, I saw kittens in the barn. Carla followed after me. Giggling in excitement, we chased after baby kittens until we were out of breath. Then they disappeared. We looked and looked, hoping for another chance for a chase but couldn't find them anywhere. Then I spotted a wooden shed nearby. Swirls of dainty white and yellow butterflies circled around it.

"Let's go see the butterflies," I told Carla. The two of us walked toward the shed, and I opened the latch. We climbed up a wooden step and saw a bench. It had two circular openings, and old newspapers and a roll of toilet paper were stacked in the middle. We sat on the open seats, waiting for the butterflies to return. Carla was tiny and petite and had to hold on with both hands to keep from falling into the hole. Then the door closed with a *thud*.

"Don't be afraid," I said. "The butterflies will open the door for us." Just then, the door did open, but instead of butterflies, we saw Uncle Joe's big smile and shiny, bright eyes.

"What are you two doing in here?" he asked. Before we could say anything, he grabbed Carla by her waist and hoisted her outside. Then he helped me down with his firm hands.

"We were visiting the butterfly house," I said.

"Butterfly house?" He laughed. "That's no butterfly house. Come on. Your mother is looking for you." He laughed. It was a comforting warm laugh.

Isn't it comforting to know that there are people in our lives who find us when we are in the wrong place and with a firm, loving hand, redirect us toward the way we should go? Christian fellowship is like that. God uses us to help each other to be a witness to his ever-faithful love. With comfort and compassion, his hand guides us toward the direction we should go.

> Praise be to the God and Father of our Lord Jesus Christ, the father of compassion and the God of all comfort, who comforts us in all our troubles, so that we can comfort those in any trouble with the comfort we ourselves have received from God.
>
> 2 Corinthians 1:3–4

A NEW LIFE

As the length of the day stretched, moisture from the heavy thick fog and inconsistent rainfall were replaced with the normal, drier air. The white silhouettes of the mountains faded away. With the changes came a hint of new life. A green, grassy carpet covered those usually chestnut-colored foothills, and wildflowers shot up in swirled patches. The weeds popped up all over our olive orchard, and the bugs appeared stretching and wiggling out of the soil. The deafening commotion in the trees came from birds defining territory and calling out for mates. Buds had begun their show as they appeared out of knarred tree branches. We experienced the transition from winter's cold to the warmth of spring, and the creation of life again unfolded before our eyes. God has woven a new season out of the winter's threads.

Now, I have been a witness to the unfolding of the miracle of life in a very personal and new way. I had a grandson, and with that desperate infant cry, I saw him seeking comfort and nourishment as he tried to make sense of the world. I examined his miniature appendages, all ten toes and fingers. One curled around my finger. He turned his head, squirming, stretching, and smelling his mother's warm breast milk—he bonds her. All systems are go.

Once again, I find our English word for "love" so limiting. We love puppies and cats, the latest shoes or a new purse design, and of course, football on Sunday afternoons. We love our cars. We love ideas and learning. We love eating a favorite meal and seeing a good movie. There is human love, such as between parent and child, husband and wife, boyfriend and girlfriend, siblings, and among friends. Now, I'm experiencing another meaning for the word: the singular love that exists between a grandparent and a grandchild. Each day I'm going to take some time to share that love, enjoy it, and let it soak in—just like the warming afternoon sun I'm feeling in the orchard. I'm going to share it with my grandson, give him a gentle but firm hug, and share with him the message that he is loved.

Even as much as I love my grandchild, I can't begin to comprehend the love that God has for us. The bond between the Creator and his creation is beyond our grasp of understanding. It's limitless, even surpassing a grandma's love.

As the Father has loved me, so I have loved you. Now remain in my love.

John 15:9

May the Lord make your love increase and overflow for each other and for everyone else, just as ours does for you.

1 Thessalonians 3:12

GOD'S COMMUNICATION SYSTEM

God is listening. He hears our prayers: our concerns, needs, desires, praises, and requests for forgiveness. It's the great communication system of all time. Talking to God is wireless technology at its best. It is the invisible landline between heaven and earth; the e-mail of the celestial Internet. No cell phone needed nor satellite installation. Prayer is the hook; it means God has our attention. Finally! We are able to turn our attention away from ourselves, from our sins, and toward God. His message is pure love. He wants to pour it over us so it fills every intricate space of our being, of our humanity. He forgives us everything. We are his chosen and become permanent dwellers in his temple; it means living in God's house. Not only do we get to live there, but we will experience the good things that permeate, surround, perfume, and infuse this heavenly temple. Huge!

So I am thankful for God's communication system. It gets me talking, and I know he's always ready to listen. I understand that my requests aren't always answered in the way I would like, and sometimes God seems silent, but it doesn't mean he's disconnected or the server is down. God's online 24/7.

Thank you, God, for this ability to communicate with you through prayer. Prayer is awesome. It turns me from myself so I can more fully experience your love for me, for humanity, and for all creation.

> Praise awaits you, O God, in Zion; to you our vows (prayers) will be fulfilled.
>
> O you who hear prayer, to you all men will come.
>
> When we were overwhelmed by sins, you forgave our transgressions.
>
> Blessed are those you choose and bring near to live in your courts!
>
> We are filled with the good things of your house, of your holy temple.
>
> Psalm 65:1–4

SAYING GOOD-BYE
TO A FRIEND

My daughter, Emily, called me, upset. Her best friend had just left. Jamie had stopped by to say a final good-bye before picking up her father at the airport. He would be helping her move to her new job and closer to his home in Dallas, Texas. Emily and Jamie had arrived in Washington D.C. about the same time. They connected easily and quickly became great friends. They had worked, shared apartments, shopped, lived through the emotional ups and downs of friendship, and explored the streets, entertainment, and restaurants for the past six years. Their friendship had survived the usual twists, turns, and drama as Emily married, moved to Maryland, and took on her role as a new mother. They took turns driving the hour plus distance to stay in touch. For Emily, this would be a huge loss. Jamie was the last of her friends to leave the area and return to her home state.

Like so many others raising families on farms or in small communities, our children find financial rewards and begin new lives far from home. Emily's life was on the East Coast. She would not be returning. I was reminded of my own sense of loss.

Still thinking about the conversation with Emily, I hurriedly drove to Port Naz, not wanting to miss their Healthy Hearts exercise program. Marie was the organizer, and I noticed that she was dressed up more for a luncheon than exercise. I told her how nice she looked.

"My best friend died this week, and I'm going to the gravesite then back here for the funeral." She held sheet music in her hand. "I'm going to sing this song. It's a song we'd sing, 'What a Day That Will Be.' We always sang it together. I wish we'd recorded it when we were younger, when our voices were better." She sighed, and as she turned away, she said, "I'm going to miss her."

We know that Jesus felt human loss too. In those final days before his death, he knew what was coming. But instead of focusing on the pain, humiliation, and torture that was to follow, he prepared one final meal to share with his friends. He knew in his absence the disciples would go through trials, grief, anger, confusion, and frustration. Without him, their world would be turned upside down and inside out. They would need each other, just as we need each other in our own time of loss. Jesus gave them an example of how they were to live together without his physical presence. He untied the hand-woven towel from around his waist, washed their feet, each in turn, teaching them humility and humbleness.

Just as the warp and weft find strength when they come together, so too would the disciples find strength through their common weaknesses. Not one would be greater than the others in this life. In their shared loss, they would find comfort. This was a gift to those Jesus loved, but we know that God's greatest gift of love was yet to come.

It was just before the Passover Feast. Jesus knew that the time had come for him to leave this world and go to the Father. Having loved his own who were in the world, he now showed them the full extent of this love.

John 13: 1

PYRAMIDS, CAMELS, AND THE FLIGHT OUT OF EGYPT

I almost threw it away because I was sure it was just another advertisement for a "special deal" or a lower mortgage rate. Then the return address caught my eye. I opened the letter and found that I had been invited to be an education delegate to Cairo, Egypt. My first response was one of suspicion. However, after much questioning and Internet searching, David and I learned that the delegation was legitimate. It was being offered through an Ambassador Program that had been founded by Dwight D. Eisenhower. After experiencing the horrors of World War II, he believed that the best way to ensure peace was for the politicians to get out of the way of everyday people. He began this foundation so that ordinary people in countries throughout the world could meet each other.

So the last week of November, after a sixteen-hour plane trip from Los Angeles and a short layover in Paris, David and I landed at the Cairo airport in Egypt with other delegates. We were greeted with warmth and great care, processed through, and on a chartered bus within the hour. Our guide introduced herself as our Egyptologist. She would be our guide to the hotel, which was located on the banks of the Nile River. Weary and tired, not knowing what to expect, and a little apprehensive, I began to feel at ease with our guide. I began to relax and enjoy my first look at Cairo at night. The bus seemed to twist and turn through the roads and highways in an organized, chaotic way, while cars were honking their way back and forth across lanes. I saw crumbled buildings alongside rebuilt apartments and tunnels of life off the side roads. There was poverty; there was wealth. So much like America, but so different too. I thought, *Isn't that what President Eisenhower intended for us to see?*

It didn't take long to check into our hotel and quickly find ourselves walking along the Nile River outside our hotel. Even though it was late, we had been told that it would be perfectly safe to take a walk and we found ourselves overlooking those ancient waters. It would be a week to remember.

That evening, as I walked along the Nile, the thought came to me that Jesus loves the people of Egypt. Their customs, language, and features were his. I was reminded that Joseph, Mary, and Jesus fled to Egypt and lived there until King Herod died. Some say they were there for less than a year, others say four.

Later that week, David found a map of their travels. Up and down the Nile they had journeyed, depending on others for their safety and welfare, much like we had done in this city of eighteen million people. Just like them, we were strangers, aliens in an unfamiliar land. I'm sure that Jesus had sent his angels to watch over us, but my thought was they've been in Egypt all along.

"Out of Egypt I called my son."

Hosea 11:1

When they had gone, an angel of the Lord appeared to Joseph in a dream. "Get up," he said, "Take the child and his mother and escape to Egypt. Stay there until I tell you, for Herod is going to search for the child to kill him."

Matthew 2:13

EQUITY

A week before I left for Egypt, I was at my physician's office for an appointment. He had been born in India but had lived and been practicing medicine in America for decades. "You are going to Muslim country," he said quite seriously, but I detected a slight twinkle in his eye. "You will find it to be quite different there."

I had no doubt that he was correct. Even as we boarded the plane in Los Angeles, I really didn't know what to expect. I had been asked to be part of the Education Equity Delegation, and I wasn't quite sure how Egyptian educators viewed "equity." As an educator in the United States, I have always thought of equity as equal access to education, especially for women and the disadvantaged. From what I had been reading in magazines and papers and watching on television, I could only guess that the hard work of equity in Egypt would point toward women.

The first day was filled with speeches from the Egyptian minister of education, well-respected Egyptian educators, and even a speech from a member of our American embassy in Cairo. The afternoon continued with meetings and a visit by teachers from a language experimental school that we would be visiting. I began to realize that we were there to listen and learn about the Egyptian educational system, not to judge, appraise, or evaluate. Not so easy for many of us.

I found the greatest difference to be religion. There are only forty-two Jewish families living in Cairo, out of a population of eighteen million. Eighty percent of the people of Egypt are Muslim and are followers of Mohammad and their holy book, the Koran. Only twenty percent are Christian, and most are Coptic Christians—one of the oldest practicing Christian groups in the world. Of that twenty percent, about two percent are Protestant Christians; Christians are clearly the minority and low on the social order.

The Muslim call for worship occurs five times a day, starting at five thirty in the morning. In past centuries, men climbed to the top of the mosques and called out prayers for the faithful to recite. Using modern technology, today, recordings of the prayers are used instead. During these calls to worship, people stop and face east. Worship and prayer is centered on this easterly direction. Even in our hotel room, we found a map compass pointing east. The last prayer of the day takes place in the evening in the privacy of homes. As a Christian, I took this opportunity to pray in my own way.

Muslim laws are enforced. Dietary laws are strict. We saw flocks of sheep and goats in the truck beds of Cairo but never saw swine. Eating pork was forbidden. Most women wore some type of head covering for religious reasons, but in some parts of Egypt, they are part of the fashion statement of teenagers and young women. Several said the heat of Egyptian sun and the coarseness of their hair, made hair difficult to style and the head coverings were helpful. They matched them with Western-style jeans, clothing, and boots. Their bodies are fully covered; maintaining modesty was a priority in this part of the world. Women were dependent on the males in their family to decide their position in society, whether a traditional religious one or a more modern one.

By the end of the week, I came to realize that the issue of equity in Egypt was more about religion: Muslim or Christian. Did a Christian child have the same educational opportunities as a Muslim child? It also had to do with economic privilege. Was a quality education available for children from poor Christian or Muslim families? Religion and poverty are the questions of equity that the Egyptian educators deal with today.

As a Christian in a predominately Christian nation, I found myself asking if we have an equity issue—a religious equity issue? I think we do, but it is not about tolerating different faiths or religions or anything to do with poverty. I think our equity issue is more about providing opportunities for the unchurched to hear the Word of God. Even in our busy working lives and with busy schedules, is there anything we can do as individuals in our Christian community to provide opportunity and access to worship and God's Word? Is there anything we can do as a church body?

> For we are God's fellow workers; you are God's field, God's building.
>
> 1 Corinthians 3:9

STEP 3:

Weaving

This is the tedious but rewarding part of the weaving process. The design of the fabric begins to reveal itself. The warp and the weft are re-created into a new whole as the shuttle holding the weft flies through the shed, tightening the threads together; it becomes something new. Christ also reworks our fabric as we build a closer relationship with him. He weaves himself into our warp and weft. We begin to understand his design for us as we join other Christians in worship and praise.

Raise the warp yarns and pass the weft yarn through the space that forms between the raised and lower yarns. That space is called the shed. Repeat until finished.

VINTAGE APRONS, TREASURED HEIRLOOMS

"Vintage." Jackie unfolded an apron. "I love vintage linens." For days we'd been rummaging through donated boxes and bags for the annual church bazaar. I stopped sorting and looked to where she stood holding a red-blue paisley print. I recognized the wrinkled cotton fabric and traditional three-square pattern. It could have been the apron assigned in home economics class in junior high school.

But, vintage? Does that make me vintage too? As I think about it, most women don't own aprons anymore, and if they do, they lie hidden under kitchen towels in the bottom of some drawer. These days I rarely wear aprons, but sometimes I put one over my frumpy sweats or housework jeans and can't help feeling a tinge of femininity, a connection to other women in my life. For many of us, aprons were part of the household landscape. If not folded and stacked into waiting piles, they hung on hooks ready for use and easily accessible.

My home economics apron had been made of 100 percent white cotton purchased at Roscoe's Five and Dime Store in downtown Sanger. I was tempted by the range of colors and prints hanging over the bolts of yardage, but my teacher had made it clear, "No prints or colors." The next year my sister's class had the choice of any print they wanted—a more modern teacher; I was envious.

My grandmother wore one, *always*. She preferred the large white ones that covered her entire body and tied in back and then in front. Her aprons had bibs. They kept her chest warm and added that little extra support as she prepared meals and did her chores. Her apron was meticulous, never a stain or blemish that I ever saw. She removed it only when she sat down at the table, hanging it on a hook near the kitchen stove.

Cooks wore oversized aprons for church sponsored dinners. Their aprons provided limited protection for their clothing as they labored over pots of boiling water, heating ovens, bowls of tossed salads, or slicing desserts. Spaghetti sauce from Italian fundraiser dinners ended up splattered all over from constant stirring and tasting. With laughter and singing, they worked at a fast pace and managed to feed everyone. By the end of the day, the messy piles of stained aprons presented a major cleaning challenge.

A neighbor was a single mom and worked as a waitress. After her death, her daughter kept her apron. Worn and faded, it has a ruffle at the bottom and a pocket where she kept her pencil and pad to take orders. Do you remember aprons with oversized, kangaroo pockets? They held bumpy handfuls of wooden clothespins.

Aprons were used for household work, to be used and reused. Once the frayed or burnt holes and stained blotches became too difficult to mend or clean, the salvaged remnants were cut up into rags for cleaning and scrubbing. Not a glamorous ending for something so indispensable.

However, not all aprons were meant for cooking and cleaning. Some were worn for special events or entertaining. My sister has Aunt Carrie's apron. Made from a thick cotton fabric, it has a large C embroidered in the center, with bouquets of flowers drifting around it. Possibly it was a gift, perhaps a wedding present and too nice to wear in the kitchen. Aprons were adorned with smocked bibs, hand-embroidered designs, rickrack-lined hems, crochet edges, and lacy, frilly finishes reflecting a femininity of the time. The tiny, even stitches and highly crafted workmanship remains impressive to this day, even under the microscope of our modern eyes and media fashion. They are vintage heirlooms.

Our lives are like those well-used aprons; they are blotched, frayed, full of imperfections and defects, and stained, with pieces missing. It's only through the message of Christ's death and resurrection that we become whole again, recycled, pure, and spotless beings. In our weakness, we become God's handiwork; we become vintage heirlooms to be cherished and treasured.

> But he said to me, "My grace is sufficient for you, for my power is made perfect in weakness."
>
> 2 Corinthians 12:9

SEA GLASS PEOPLE

We left the cold, valley fog behind and ended up in Cayucos for the weekend. We rented a room with an ocean view and spent the first hour on the balcony, taking in the sunshine and watching the waves pulling in and out. As the low tide began, the waves began receding, and a small beach appeared. Immediately, people of all sizes, ages, and shapes began appearing. Some were walking their dogs, while others stopped to examine a pile of tangled wood and rusted iron. However, most of them seemed to be examining the sand, looking for something. They were picking at stones or rocks—maybe agates? Maybe shells? They certainly were selective, bending and stooping as needed, poking the wet sand with makeshift sticks. Some had buckets, others held plastic bags, and a few used their pockets. Whatever it was they were looking for, they seemed satisfied; I was content to watch and guess at what they were doing.

Later that day, David stopped by the lobby of the motel and asked about the activity on the beach. He called me to join him so I could hear the answer myself. The woman behind the counter answered, "Sea glass." She brought out a glass bowl from another room. It was halfway filled with small, odd-shaped pieces of glass that she had found on the beach. Their rough edges had been rubbed smooth by ocean sediments and pounding waves. The colors were remarkable. There were several shades of green and white pieces from what had been broken glass bottles, but there were also an unusual number of turquoise blue ones and other odd colors.

"People from all over the world collect them, from beaches all over the world," she said. "The last sea glass convention was in Boston." Then she smiled. "Let me show you what I found the other day." She pulled out of her bowl a blue marble with a white swirl through it. I held it in my hand. It was not perfectly round—tiny indentions had formed where chunks had been broken off—but even these were as polished and smooth as the rest of the glass pieces in her bowl. The blue color had softened; the white was the color of clouds. It was beautiful, refined.

"And what about that pile of wood and rusted iron on the beach?" I asked.

"Some shipwreck. Some think it sunk out here somewhere during the forties, but no one seems to know for sure. The currents have been changing, moving the sand around. Who knows where it's coming from? Some people found coins, an Indian arrowhead or two. Someone even found an Indian whistle that came from Mexico. Imagine all the way here from Mexico." She paused. "But the sea glass. That's the best."

Aren't we like the sea glass that washes up on the shores? We are the shipwrecked, the broken, the lost, and the discarded people of this world. Even as we break apart, crash, and shatter into so many pieces, Jesus takes us and transforms us into something new.

We become polished and smooth and something to be valued. We are alive in Christ's love.

> And we, who with unveiled faces all reflect the Lord's glory, are being transformed into his likeness with ever-increasing glory, which comes from the Lord, who is the Spirit.
>
> 2 Corinthians 3:18

> The Lord Jesus Christ, who by the power that enables him to bring everything under his control, will transform our lowly bodies so that they will be like his glorious body.
>
> Philippians 3:21

FRESH START

It was Friday afternoon, the last half hour of the school week. The children sitting so quietly in my classroom were serving detention because of missing homework assignments, incomplete class work or wrong choices. Several were more than a few assignments behind and were regulars. They were used to the routine, having long since given up on excuses and pretexts. Three girls had been involved in a shouting match this week, which led to some major pushing and shoving. A boy had cheated on a spelling test. One of the girls had torn off the name of another child's homework and written her name on it instead. She didn't want to get into trouble for not having her homework done. This reasoning made sense to her; a child's logic. Another boy had been in tears as he tried to talk his way out of two late homework assignments. He had argued that he had left them at home. "They were done," he repeated to me. He had just forgotten them at home. I reminded him that he had been forgetting them since Monday. Now he sat quietly, working on his spelling sentences, resigned to the situation.

I quietly walked to the board in front of the room. There I checked over the list of students serving detention. Everyone was here. Satisfied, I walked through the rows of students, monitoring their progress on assignments. Soon, a noisy line of students began to form outside my door. These were the students who had been in other rooms working on various activities of their choice. As I dismissed the detention group, I asked one of the regulars if he would like to erase the detention names on the front board.

"Can I?" He smiled.

"Yes," I answered. "Everyone gets to start all over. Everyone gets a fresh start on Monday." I knew he would probably be here next Friday afternoon, but I didn't give up on him. Sometimes even the regulars will surprise you. There is always the possibility.

Christ too offers us the chance for a new beginning, but his offer is available all year long, in every season, and with every breath we take. He offers real possibilities for change because he invites us to follow him in a very personal way. Even as we stumble, he is always there to help us and encourage us to do better. The best part is that he never gives up on us. There is always hope.

The Lord delights in those who fear him, who put their hope in his unfailing love.

Psalm 147:11

FOOTSTEPS

Where do you travel? Where does your journey lead you? What footsteps do you leave behind?

We took our fifth graders to the annual Tulare County Symphony last month. The Buck Shaffer Auditorium was filled to capacity with ten- and eleven-year-old children from all over the county. Their excitement was obvious with their noisy voices, lively shouts, and vigorous sounds of bouncing seats; however, when the conductor raised his arms to begin, silence flowed out over the audience in waves. The quiet seconds were soon replaced with the blending sounds of strings, percussions, woodwinds, and trumpets. Children who could hardly sit still before the concert were now mesmerized by the rhythms, tones, and tempo of the music. One of my students, whose attention span was equal to the movements of a worker ant when it came to class work, was riveted to the scene before him. He didn't move a muscle except to give me a quick side-glance and a big approving smile. I wish that those wonderful performers could have shared that moment with me. These musicians had taken off time from work and busy lives to share their gifts with these children.

Nancy works at the Circle J-Norris Ranch. Her expertise is biology and sharing the love of nature with both children and adults. On hot spring days, she can be found with a group of ten-year-olds, mucking through pond water to capture a tadpole or other water creatures. The children's delight is heightened as they examine microscopic river life under childproof microscopes. Long after the life-forms are returned to the river and the children have returned to their homes, they remember the abundance and richness of life that they have seen. Someday, Nancy wants to return to Africa to share her knowledge with people on that continent. I think her greatest work may be here in our Sierra Nevada foothills.

Over fifteen hundred people are fed Thanksgiving Day meals. Members from over twenty-eight local churches come together to prepare, package, and deliver meals each year. The organization and implementation of such an enterprise would test the skills of a CEO from a major corporation. Our people do it with prayer and out of Christian love for others. Also, there must be a special blessing on those who stay behind to clean up especially the mass of sticky footprints spattered across the kitchen floor.

A friend spends her birthday working in a homeless shelter. Children's Sunday school and teen activities, bazaars, and fundraisers are manned with silent, diligent workers. A teacher spends his break playing football with a group of active students. Parents volunteer their time to serve hot chocolate to 400 elementary school children. A retired senior volunteers time at the Boys and Girls Club. Though their eyes grow tired easily, women come together to sew a quilt that is raffled off at a fundraiser for the community. Others buy tickets or donate money. Each footstep leads to another.

All these people come together, each one like a fiber on the loom, becoming part of God's handiwork. They are creating something bigger than themselves.

Where do you leave your footsteps? You might not truly understand the impact you leave behind. Jesus does. You are his worker.

> A new command I give you: Love one another. As I have loved you, so you must love one another. By this all men will know that you are my disciples, if you love one another.
>
> John 13:34–35

WELL WATER AND THE BROKEN PUMP

Those of you who have grown up in the San Joaquin Valley are familiar with the vineyards and orchards in places like Reedley, Sanger, Dinuba, Parlier, and Clovis. Water remains the life blood for farming and this way of life. During those plus 100-degree temperatures of summer, water can mean the difference between crop failure and success. Water comes from underground wells, pumped to the surface with motors. Sometimes, they break, or a well runs dry.

You might have known my uncle Aldo or someone very much like him. He fixed pumps and helped to drill wells. Sometimes, we have to grow up and experience life before we can really appreciate people in our lives. My uncle was such a person.

There were five children in our family and four in his. We visited back and forth during the year but especially on weekends. I especially remember one Saturday evening. For some reason, the girls were inside when we all heard the phone ring. My aunt looked at my uncle. He sighed, got up from the couch, and went into the kitchen to answer the phone. He had just finished a long day of work in three-digit heat.

"Hello," he answered the phone and then listened for a minute. "Okay, I'll be there as soon as I can."

"Pump's out, no water for his trees." He explained to the other adults. He left the room and then returned wearing a clean pair of blue overalls, slipping the metal clasps into place over his shoulders. He found his hat. Outside, he took off his shoes and replaced them with his iron-brown working boots. They were still thick with mud, and he banged them together making a mess of dried dirt, which fell all over the sidewalk. He drove off in the company truck.

I am reminded of this story because we are currently farming olives in the south valley and dependent on a well. Living on five acres of olives, we are not on a city waterline, and when the electricity is turned off or the pump isn't working, water isn't available for our household needs or to irrigate our orchard. Without water, life becomes complicated. Just recently, we ran out of water. The pump wasn't working.

That evening, I was washing a few stray dishes and commented to David. "The water pressure seems a little low." He went outside to check the water filter and the pump, located several yards from the house. He quickly returned with a resigned look on his face.

"I'll try this pump company." He reached for a business card. "They're closer than the others. They're small, but I've heard they do good work."

He made the phone call, and the owner of the company said that he would be there in about an hour. A couple of hours later, he drove into the driveway with his truck. He examined the pump. Apparently, the pump equipment was over thirty years old. "A dinosaur," he had told us. "Your motor might be going out, but for now, I think I can fix it."

He returned to his truck, found a part, and replaced it in less than fifteen minutes. Relief! I always feel so vulnerable when the water is turned off and feel so grateful there are people in this world who can fix pumps.

About a week later, I was out near the pump and thought the motor was running more than it should have been. David checked several times that evening and ended up calling the same man to come back and check on the pump. Several days later, after leaving messages with the answering service and with promises of returning, David called another company.

After work the next day, I drove into the driveway and parked behind yet another company's truck. David greeted me with, "No water for at least a day. Had to order some parts." Just then, the worker got into his truck and waved good-bye. "Parts should be in tomorrow. Let you know if they don't show."

David then went on to explain that the part, which had been replaced originally, had somehow overheated and was burning through some heavy cardboard type material.

David showed me the part. I was amazed.

He added, "I explained to him what had happened, how the other company hadn't returned my calls."

The man who had just left had told David, "Oh, yeah, that guy. He doesn't like working the small jobs. He would rather work the big jobs, the important jobs. You can see that."

The next day, I arrived home to running water, and the first thing I did was take a shower. A shower can be such a luxury!

My delight was short-lived. In less than a week, the water stopped completely. The little water that managed to get through the pipes was mixed with a blackish sludge.

"Either we struck oil or the motor went out?" I said.

"My guess is the motor," David said. "I'll call him back."

David called the second company. "Be out there as soon as I can. Right now, I'm drilling a well. People here don't have any water at all. Well's dry. May have to drill several hundred feet. Happening all over. It's the drought."

We knew he wanted our business but we soon realized that he wouldn't be able to get to our place for at least another week.

We called a third, larger company. They came out the next day. Sure enough, the motor wasn't working. It'd have to be pulled up out of the ground, pipes included, wiring, and everything had to be replaced. There was also the question of the water table. Was there water down there or would they have to drill deeper?

Does that sound expensive? It was. But in two days, we had a new motor, pipes, and electrical wiring. They measured our water level at fifty feet. So we didn't have to worry about digging a new well after all. The men working on the pump were impressed with our water table especially during this drought. We learned later that a few years ago, the water table around us had been at twenty-nine feet. It had dropped over twenty feet.

Again, our relief was short-lived. About a week later, I was watering our garden, and the water stopped. "David," I called. "Did you turn off the water?" I was hoping that he would say yes, but he didn't.

It was 4:30 on a Friday afternoon when he called the third company again. These things always happen on a Friday afternoon. One of the men who had worked on the project managed to drive over and check everything. He was mad. "It's a brand new motor. Something is wrong with the motor," he said, shaking his head. "I think it's a short. All of our trucks have jobs tomorrow, but I'll see what we can do. A brand-new motor, I can't believe it."

No water! So David filled up plastic containers with water from the pool for flushing, I bought large plastic bottles of fresh water and got out the baby wipes. We would go out for dinner. We had this routine down. I couldn't imagine what we do after weeks of no water.

Fortunately for us, a crew of two men showed up early the next day. It was Saturday morning and should have been their day off. Instead, they had volunteered to work on this job. By 2:30 in the afternoon, they had finished. A seal on the motor had broken, and water had seeped through. But we had water again. I couldn't thank them enough.

So I know now that besides being a great person, my uncle had a heart for people. He would give up his weekends, his family life, and free time so that others could have water. No one farmer was more important than another. No one client was worth more than another. It's the same with Christ.

Do nothing out of selfish ambition or vain conceit, but in humility consider others better than your-selves. Each of you should look not to your own interests, but also to the interest of others.

Philippians 2: 3–4

DEAR MOM:
I MISS YOU

Dear Mom,

I miss you a lot and I want to go with you. How are you? I'm good. Say hi to my cousins for me. I love you.

When I go with you, I'm going to have a lot of fun with you. I am happy because you are going to have a baby. I hope it is a girl and I could help you take care of her. I hope she is pretty and looks a little like me. I will see you in the summer. Bye.

Love,
Me

P.S. I miss you a lot.

This was a letter written by a ten-year-old girl to her mom. At the time she wrote this letter, she was living with her dad. He was also raising two other younger children by himself. The girl's mom had started a new life in another state.

As I read this letter, I thought to myself how often human love fails us. How frail our human love is. Just as children seek unconditional love from parents, adults seek that same kind of commitment from others. We are often disappointed; human beings are far from perfect, just like some of my weaving projects.

Our ability to express our love for each other is dented and broken as the world is dented and broken. So we must learn to seek that love which comes to us through the sacrifice of Jesus, who died on the cross for us. That is how we truly learn to love each other. That kind of love never disappoints.

> I pray that out of his glorious riches he may strengthen you with power through his Spirit in your inner being, so that Christ may dwell in your hearts through faith. And I pray that you, being rooted and established in love, may have power, together with all the saints, to grasp how wide and long and high and deep is the love of Christ, and to know this love that surpasses knowledge—that you my be filled to the measure of all the fullness of God.
>
> Ephesians 3:16–19

WHO'S THE BOSS?

"What is a principal?" I asked my class.

The children answered, "The principal is the boss of the school."

"Yes," I said. Children see things in a very simplistic, uncomplicated way.

As a teacher, I view the principal more as an air traffic controller than a boss. A principal organizes the yearly flight plans, knowing that at a moment's notice, planes can be grounded and put on hold due to emergency precautions and an unexpected crisis. There are broken sewer lines or busted bathroom plumbing. Maybe the cafeteria is short fifty lunches or the school's server goes down. Lockdowns and suspicious-person warnings can keep students in their classrooms for hours. Children can derail a perfectly good flight schedule in less than fifteen minutes on the playground during recess. On other days, the principal can expect a crash and burn from a teacher or two. The district office has directives and guidelines, which can often call for creative divisive maneuvers. Parents seem to hold out for the perfect day to plan an unexpected ambush. Angry statements like, "Why can't I pick up my child? I don't need a court order to see my own child," can set up work stoppage.

There are break-ins, faulty alarm systems, and graffiti. Usually, these occur on weekends or days off.

"What day off?" the principal asks. There is never a day off when one is trafficking a school.

With so many people going in so many directions at once and so many fires to put out, a principal must wonder, sometimes, who's really the boss. Who's really in control? A little bit of prayer goes a long way in the principal's office.

No matter our station in life, we can never be totally in control. We need to give the idea of control to the Lord. He is ready to take our burdens whatever they might be and help us make the best decisions that we are able. He is the real boss.

> I urge, then, first of all, that requests, prayers, intercession and thanksgiving be made for everyone— for kings and all those in authority, that we may live peaceful and quiet lives in all godliness and holiness.
>
> 1 Timothy 2:1–2

PERSONALIZED BATS IN LOUISVILLE, KENTUCKY

For David, one of the highlights of our road trip this summer was a visit to the Louisville Slugger Factory in Louisville, Kentucky. They've been making wooden baseball bats for 125 years. David's family always said that he grew up with a baseball in one hand and a bat in the other, playing for hours in makeshift baseball fields until the sun set. We couldn't bypass this part of Americana or a reminder of his youth.

The morning of our visit, we programmed our newly-acquired navigation system to guide us to the factory. We named it Hallie after Hal in the movie, *Space Odyssey 2001*. She told us where to go in an unrelenting voice and without any opportunity for questions or dialogue.

In all fairness, Hallie did a good job guiding us over the bridges and interstates of Louisville to a parking garage adjacent to the factory. Once inside the three-story brick building, we found the counter where David ordered a personalized bat. It would take an hour and a half. While we were waiting, we visited the museum filled with displays of baseball memorabilia and took the factory tour. The guide showed us the pile of billets made from northern white ash (they looked like rolling pins without handles to me). Bending over a wooden billet, a worker demonstrated how bats were hand-formed on lathes before technology was introduced. Today, one bat takes thirty seconds to make. We saw the entire process, all computerized, of course. So many choices: weight, wood, shape, shades of tans and browns, varnishing, emblems, names, leagues, and personal etchings. There were wooden bats for little leagues, schools, colleges, semi-pro, and the major leagues.

Once a year, pink bats are made and then donated to major league baseball players. They, in turn, auction these autographed bats to raise money for breast cancer research. Of course, the more famous the player, the more money collected. To date, over $700,000 has been raised.

Toward the end of the tour, we were guided to a separate part of the factory where bats for the major league players are made. They take a little more time: forty-five seconds. Behind us were bins of bats labeled with past and current players names, like Ruth, Gehrig, Williams, Jeters, and A-Rod. Major league teams purchase their players' bats, while from the Triple A on down, the ball players pay for their own bats. The time went by quickly, and before long, David picked up his bat. He had chosen the Yankee logo etched into the middle and "David's Special" on the top. I held the bat. It was surprisingly heavy, and I noticed the fine grain of the wood.

"It is special." I smiled back at him.

Each one of us is a "God's Special." We are his creation. Like the bats formed at the factory, we are a special order in God's plan. We have our own shades of color, weights, measurements, varnishing, and personal signature. In spite of their differences, the bats all start out with the same wood. With God, we're all the same too—created in his image. We share God's life in us. We share God's love for us. God sent his only Son to die on a wooden cross so we could know how very special we are. It is his personalized gift to each one of us.

> For the word of the LORD is right and true; he is faithful in all he does. The LORD loves righteousness and justice, the earth is full of his unfailing love.
>
> Psalm 33:4–5

> For I am convinced that neither death nor life, neither angels nor demons, neither the present nor the future, nor any powers, neither height nor depth, nor anything else in all creation, will be able to separate us from the love of God that is in Christ Jesus our Lord.
>
> Romans 8:38–39

UNCHURCHED

"Dad, it's been a year. We promised to wait a year, like you asked."

Emma stood facing her father. He watched the determination in her face. Even as he searched for the slightest sign of wavering, he knew there wouldn't be any compromise.

"Emma." Ahmed softly quieted her and faced her father. "Mr. Brocklen, I love your daughter. We have been engaged for a year now; we waited a year, just as you asked. Nothing has changed between us. Your daughter wants an American wedding, a Christian wedding. I have agreed. We would like to get married and ask that you give us your blessing."

Ahmed was handsome, polite, and respectful. Born in the Middle East, he had come to America as a college student. After graduation, he became an American citizen, started a successful business, and now owned several companies in the area. He drove the best cars and owned several homes. If Emma married him, she would never want for anything material.

"You understand why we hesitate?" he answered Ahmed. "It is because you are Muslim, and Emma has been raised a Christian."

His wife looked over at him puzzled, surprised again. The first time he had shared his concern, she'd been astonished and almost choked in surprise. They'd been married in a Christian church but had never been members. She'd tried to convince him to attend church with her, any church. He did for a while, but then she'd found herself going alone. His reasons were the usual. "You can find God anywhere; you don't need a church. The service is boring, doesn't mean anything to me. They just want your money; church people are hypocritical." She'd taken the girls for a while, but he hadn't encouraged them. She'd become weary of the battle, his remarks, and church put-downs; and now, she went alone.

"Yes, I understand," he answered. "My parents have forbidden me to marry your daughter too; she's not of my faith. My father told me that if I marry Emma, none of my family will attend. They'd never attend such a wedding."

They were surprised to hear this. Ahmed and Emma had visited his family the past summer. Emma had been impressed with his family. "Mom, the people are so kind. The children are respectful, and teenagers would never talk back. They dress modestly. Yes, they cover their heads but only on the streets. It's more of a fashion statement." She added, "Our beliefs are not so different. Did you know that they recognize Jesus? Only he's a prophet. They even teach about Mary and Joseph. Isn't that amazing?" Her naivety was shocking even to her father.

"We found a minister who will marry us," Emma stated.

"Too many differences," several ministers had told them. "Not only extreme differences in religion, but culture too." One minister agreed, but only if they attended counseling. They didn't see the necessity.

Emma continued, "We're having a September wedding. We found a place in the wine country. Arrangements have been made. Everything is paid for; Ahmed took care of everything." Silence followed. "We want you to be there. Dad, I want you to give me away," Emma spoke softly.

"What about your parents, Ahmed?" he asked.

"No. My father has made his decision. But after the wedding, we're flying to my home to stay with my family." He paused and then added, "We will be back before Christmas."

"I'd never miss Christmas with you," Emma said. "I would never want to miss the Christmas tree, the presents, the decorations."

"Celebrate the birth of Jesus?" her mom added.

"Oh, yeah, that too," she answered.

"Easter too?"

"Well, yes, but why Easter?"

> Train a child in the way he should go, and when he is old he will not turn from it.
>
> Proverbs 22:6

CONFLICT

Iwo Jima is an island of the Japanese Volcano Island chain located in the Pacific Ocean, 1,200 kilometers from Tokyo. Once a year, the Japanese government allows a limited number of people to visit the island; most are World War II veterans, family members, or historians. However, few veterans choose to return.

This past July, about a thousand of us had a chance to sail by this historic island on our way to view the solar eclipse in the China Sea. As the island came into view, passengers lined the port side of the ship to view this World War II iconic piece of real estate. We saw a relatively small island, a total of ten square miles, four and one half miles long by two and one half miles wide. Docile and quiet, the only disturbance comes from the sounds of waves crashing against the beach and bird calls. Bright green grass covers the once broken ground. Human activity was clearly absent. A single volcanic caldera, Mount Suribachi, stands on one end of the island. The rest is flat. Entrances to wartime bunkers and volcanic tunnels that the Japanese enlarged and connected during the war were out of sight. Today, an airstrip and tall metal poles are the only hint of civilization.

It was here that US Navy ships provided cover as American soldiers charged the island held by Japanese troops during World War II. The battle lasted From February 19 until March 26 of 1945. Most of the 21,000 Japanese soldiers fought to the death, only a few thousand were captured. Americans suffered 25,000 causalities with nearly 7,000 deaths. Such a small piece of land for so many deaths, so many deaths.

We see through history's binoculars this huge conflict erupting over a little known and seemingly unimportant piece of land. Such an insignificant island decided the fate of a much larger issue—the beginning of the end of World War II. In our lives too, it is often the small things that drive and fuel the biggest conflicts and often determine our decisions.

Before the battle was over, the famous photograph, *Raising the Flag on Iwo Jima* had been taken. It became a symbol of heroic soldiers fighting the Japanese army and winning. Later, even that event would become surrounded in controversy. A battle has many perspectives; one view is never more definitive or clearer than another.

A survivor of this battle was on our cruise and offered to share his story with us. He had been a teenager when he enlisted in the navy. "It was the right thing to do," he told us. "They didn't really check your age." He went on to describe some of his experiences on board navel ships at that time, but only bits and pieces of his memory from the battle itself and loss of those around him. One final question came from the audience.

"So how do you feel about Japanese people today? After such a terrible battle, is it possible to forgive?"

He smiled at the question; the room became quiet in anticipation of his answer. "Well, let me tell you in a simple way. I have a granddaughter who is half-Japanese."

> He will judge between the nations and will settle disputes for many people. They will beat their swords into plowshares and their spears into pruning hooks. Nation will not take up sword against nation, nor will they train for war anymore.
>
> Isaiah 2:4

> Then Peter came to Jesus and asked, "Lord, how many times shall I forgive my brother when he sins against me? Up to seven times?" Jesus answered, "I tell you, not seven times but seventy-seven times."
>
> Matthew 18:21–22

A GOD MOMENT

It was a God moment. It had been just one week ago that we had sailed out of the port of Tianjin after a three-hour bus ride from Beijing. Now on July 22, I was standing on a deck of a cruise ship with over a thousand other people. We were in the middle Pacific Ocean waiting to see a total solar eclipse. The moon's orbit was as close to the earth as possible, and the earth's orbit was at the furthest point from the sun. It would be the longest eclipse of the century, lasting over six minutes.

Except for a few clouds on the horizon, the sky had cleared. It would be the only clear day of the cruise. Later, we learned that groups in Shangri and southern Japan were not able to witness the eclipse because of cloudy and overcast skies. We held on to protective eye coverings so that we could look directly at the sun. There had been many warnings and reminders that looking directly into the sun causes blindness. I had some idea of what to expect. I felt I was ready. After all, I had been teaching students about eclipses for years. But I was not prepared for what I would see.

As the moon's shadow began passing over the sun, a crescent shape began to appear over the sun's surface. Gradually, the sky began to darken, the clouds took on eerie dark shades of orange colors, and the temperature of the air dropped drastically. Venus and Mercury appeared. The corona of the sun encircled the moon's dark shadow. It blasted out spears of light, preventing total darkness. We laughed and shouted in joyful exuberance.

The moon began its reverse motion. A tiny halo of light suddenly turned into a ring around the moon's shadow. A bulging diamond of light appeared at the tip of the ring. It was unlike any ring I had ever seen. Then just as my brain caught up with the messages streaming from my eyes, the diamond in the ring explored into a brilliant light. The sun began reclaiming its place in the sky. At that instance, I knew that I had been a witness to a tiny glimpse of creation.

It took us almost a week to get back to Beijing and our flight home. In two and a half weeks, we had visited parts of China, South Korea, and Japan. We had sailed past Pacific Islands, which included a brief sail around Iwo Jima. We had experienced diverse lifestyles, unusual food textures and tastes, languages, writing, money exchanges and cultural taboos, similarities and differences. The solar eclipse still stopped me in my mental tracks. We were tired, exhausted, and filled with so many emotions. It was mind and body overload.

As I sat on the plane ready to return home, I noticed a young woman wearing a diamond ring—an engagement ring. In our culture, it is the symbol of a personal relationship between two people. It is a commitment to each other. In thinking about the diamond ring I had seen during the eclipse, I was reminded that the Lord desires an intimate relationship between himself and his people. He is the groom, and we, his church, are his bride. If the solar eclipse was any indication, the wedding will be spectacular.

> Let us rejoice and be glad and give him glory!
>
> For the wedding of the Lamb has come, and his bride has made herself ready.
>
> Revelation 19:7

FROM A SEEDLING
TO A CABBAGE

Last March, Grandma Lucy received an urgent call from her granddaughter.

"Grandma, Grandma," Rebekah called. "The teacher gave us a seedling to plant. We have to find a good place to plant it. Can Grandpap find a place in the yard?"

"Don't you want to grow it in your own yard?"

"No, no, it will just die. I'll forget to water it."

After much discussion, Rebekah showed up at Grandpap's with a small container in her hand. It held a single seedling. With quiet patience and deliberation, the two found a perfect spot among the flowers in the back of the house where it would face the eastern sun. First, they dug out a carefully formed hole, lifted the plant gently out of its container, and cautiously placed it in its new place. They packed the dirt down around its stem, added some mulch, watered it, and then Grandpap made a ring of slug and snail pellets to keep any unwanted intruders away. Satisfied, Rebekah left for home confident that her young seedling was in very good hands.

Between the morning rays of sunlight, good soil, and the automatic sprinklers, the seedling thrived and flourished. It grew into an impressive head of cabbage. Finally, the day arrived when the children were to return their cabbage plants to the classroom. In preparation for the big day, Rebekah and Grandpap ceremoniously cut the head off its stem. The outside leaves were tough and thick. Maybe the inside would be the same? No one was quite sure; after all, this was their first cabbage plant. Cutting it open would have to wait. They placed it on a scale; it weighed nine pounds. Next, they measured its circumference, which turned out to be an impressive forty-two inches. "Do you think our cabbage turned out okay?" Rebekah questioned.

"I think it's just fine, but you'll just have to wait until you see what the other cabbage plants look like."

Rebekah returned after school with her prize cabbage beaming from ear to ear. "So, how did it go, Rebekah?"

"Half of the plants died. Some had cabbages, but they were tiny and looked funny. Some were okay, but mine was the biggest and the heaviest." She smiled again. "Thank you, Grandpap." The real harvest wasn't the cabbage, but in that smile.

What kind of cabbage would you produce if given a seedling? Would you be willing to put in the time, patience, and energy over several months even for a grandchild? It's the same in our Christian life. We are offered the seed, but it's what we do with it that determines our harvest.

> This is the meaning of the parable; the seed is the word of God. Those along the path are the ones who hear, and then the devil comes and takes away the word from their hearts, so that they may not

believe and be saved. Those on the rock are the ones who receive the word with joy when they hear it, but they have no root. They believe for a while, but in the time of testing they fall away. The seed that fell among thorns stands for those who hear, but at they go on their way they are choked by life's worries, riches, and pleasures, and they do not mature. But the seed on good soil stands for those with a noble and good heart, who hear the word, retain it, and by persevering produce a crop.

Luke 8:11–15

BUT, LORD, HOW CAN WE FEED SO MANY?

Whatever our individual feelings and views concerning immigration issues, the reality is that we are talking about between eleven and twelve million people. Governments on both sides of the border struggle with the complexity of the situation and often seem irresponsible and out of touch. The cost for education, medical, social services, and prisons impacts the budgets of poor and wealthy states alike. Solutions are evasive and complicated; feelings on both sides of the issue reveal frustration and anger. When faced with such an overwhelming problem, it helps to be able to see an individual, a single fiber on the loom but connected to all the other fibers—part of a larger piece.

Sometimes, when we travel, we lose track of what's going on in the world. So, after checking into a motel in New Mexico this past summer, we turned on the television to a local station. A newsperson was running a piece on immigrants and interviewed a Mexican man staying in a shelter in New Mexico. Along with his wife and family, he had crossed the border and had been living in Arizona working as a car mechanic for the past seven years. He had a good paying job and was able to provide a good life for his family in Arizona. Now, he had to leave his job and try to find work elsewhere because he had entered the United States illegally.

"I'm trying to find work. I want to be able to feed my family," he said in Spanish.

"How is your family doing now?

"They're okay. We have enough money to last us a few more months."

"What will you do if you can't find work in New Mexico?"

"I will keep looking; maybe another state. I'm a good worker."

"And if you don't find work?"

"I might have to go back to Mexico, but there is nothing there for us. The violence, the poverty. I used to think I could save enough money and return to Mexico; open my own business. No more."

Then the camera switched over to a spokeswoman in charge of the Catholic shelter where the interview was taking place. "We provide a few days of shelter and food for those crossing the border or who have need. Lately, we have been helping a lot of people from Arizona looking for jobs. So many people, mostly men. But all we can do is offer food and shelter. New Mexico is a poor state, we don't have jobs; our resources are limited. We do what we can."

That is all the Lord asks us to do. He asks us to do what we can, no matter how insignificant we think our contribution and overwhelming the problem. Give him the glory, and he will do the rest.

> When Jesus looked up and saw a great crowd coming toward him, he said to Philip, "Where shall we buy bread for these people to eat?" He asked this only to test him, for he already had in mind what he was going to do.
>
> Philip answered him, "Eight months' wages would not buy enough bread for each one to have a bite!"
>
> Another of his disciples, Andrew, Simon Peter's brother, spoke up, "Here is a boy with five small barley loaves and two small fish, but how far will they go among so many?"
>
> Jesus said, "Have the people sit down." There was plenty of grass in that place and the men sat down, about five thousand of them. Jesus then took the loaves, gave thanks, and distributed to those who were seated as much as they wanted. He did the same with the fish.
>
> When they had all had enough to eat, he said to his disciples, "Gather the pieces that are left over. Let nothing be wasted."
>
> So they gathered them and filled twelve baskets with the pieces of the five barley loaves left over by those who had eaten.
>
> John 6:5–13

STEP 4:

Finishing Touches

After all the steps have been completed and I have finished my latest weaving project, I gently cut off the ends from the loom and take a few minutes to enjoy what I have created. I hold the new fabric in my hands and stare at it with my eyes. I listen to its form and shape. No talking allowed.

With God, it's not only about following a process, but rather the act of being with God in a still and quiet place. Along with worship, prayer, fellowship, and Bible study, we add meditation. As we practice at being still, we begin to understand the fabric that God is weaving in each one of us. It's about letting go of our self-will and surrendering fully knowing that his design for us is wonderfully made.

With my weaving, it's time to begin a new project; but with God, we are his ongoing project.

Remove the finished woven piece by cutting the warp yarns from the back and front of the loom. It might start to unravel so it is important to tie the ends into knots. Then unwind the piece from the front beam. Remove the piece.

The unwoven warp yarns can be left as is and used as fringe or shaped into tassels. The ends can also be trimmed and hemmed. Then the final piece needs to be washed and dried. Wool needs to be blocked. The difference in the feel and color of the material, before and after washing, is always an unexpected surprise.

The finished project is now ready to be used unless the weaver decides to create something more complicated like a piece of clothing. Cutting lines need to be drawn onto the fabric first. The lines need to be reinforced with stitching on both sides before cutting along the lines with scissors or other cutting tool, Then the pieces are sewn together forming the finished product.

HAULING BOXES
TO TEXAS

No sooner had we returned from our daughter's wedding in Maryland than we were busy with our son's move to the Houston, Texas, where he had accepted a position. He had been a graduate student for the past seven years and had accumulated very little that was worth moving. He sold his surfboard and got a good price for his car. So after a morning of sorting and discarding, we managed to get everything packed into eighteen good-sized, cardboard boxes, which fit snugly into the back of our Ford truck.

The three of us were soon on the road with most of Nate's worldly possessions in the back of the truck. We decided to drive south over the Ridge Route and connect with Highway 10, which would take us all the way to Texas. As we entered Arizona, we were reminded of the possibility of summer lightning storms and managed to stay ahead of a threatening one all day. Our first day ended in Tucson with most of the boxes stashed into the cab of the truck, and the rest stacked on a luggage carrier that fit next to a vacant wall in the motel room.

We were tired and hungry and decided to wait until morning to figure out the best way to protect the boxes from thunderstorms. My first thought the next morning was to check the weather. "Maybe the thunderstorms had passed?" I found out that it wasn't going to be that easy. The manager of the motel said rain was forecasted for the rest of the week from Arizona to New Mexico.

"A tarp would work," someone suggested. Good idea, but we agreed that would mean giving up valuable time searching for a store that carried what we needed. We finally came up with the idea of plastic trash bags and duct tape. We loaded up the boxes into the bed of the truck and drove out of the motel parking lot, again just ahead a threatening storm. About five miles out on the highway, we stopped at a combination gas station and convenience store and found the extra heavy duty trash bags and tape we needed. So I jumped up onto the truck bed while Nate and David stood at the gate. The three of us double bagged each one of those boxes, taping close any openings. We were just driving off when the rainstorm hit us. I kept a careful watch from the backseat of the truck checking for any loose pieces of plastic. After another stop or two to check the bags, we finally relaxed. The bag idea was a good one. It was a keeper.

We confidently drove through Arizona and New Mexico until we finally arrived in El Paso. Its border partner, Juarez, Mexico, could be seen just across the Rio Grande. Juarez appeared to be the poor relative. The river separated more than just real estate; it separated two different ways of life.

Then I looked at the map and announced that it was 700 miles to San Antonio. Groans form the front seat. There was another groan when we realized that we had lost two hours to time zone changes. So we decided to stop at one of the small dots on the map for the night. The small dot turned out to be Fort Stockton.

The motel was almost full, but we managed to get one of the last two rooms available. It was around seven in the evening, and a warm breeze was blowing. I didn't notice any children, but there were several men standing outside talking, strangers connected by a stay-over in a motel in the middle of South Texas. Their small trucks and vans were labeled "Forestry Service" or with the logos of engineering or construction companies. A single big rig was parked nearby.

We began our routine of unpacking the boxes and putting them in the cab of the truck. The motel didn't have an elevator, so we ended up hauling the remaining boxes upstairs. I'm sure that we were entertainment for the other guests. Maybe they were playing a mental guessing game with the contents of our boxes?

Dinner that night came from the snack bag I had packed. We found a mini-mart and bought some cheese, chips, and salsa to add to our tomatoes, avocados and nuts. The microwave in the room was great for making nachos.

The next day we made it to Houston. The boxes stayed with us in a motel room for four more nights. Finally, he was able to move into his apartment; so for one last time, we loaded and unloaded those boxes. The boxes were now ready to open and unpack. They were safe and where they needed to be. I felt the same way about Nate. He would be living 1,500 miles away from us but he was in a place that he needed to be. I knew that the Lord had prepared this place for him and his boxes too.

> Be joyful always; pray continually, give thanks in all circumstances, for this is God's will for you in Christ Jesus.
>
> I Thessalonians 5:16–18

TRUSTING IN A SCHOOL BUS DRIVER

It wasn't until we had passed two school buses parked off the shoulder of the Grapevine going south on I-5, that I realized how skillful our school bus driver had been. We left our elementary school at 6:30 in the morning on our way to the Reagan Presidential Library in Simi Valley. The first part of the trip had been on Highway 65. Staying well within the speed limit for school buses, we soon had an extended line of frustrated cars and trucks behind us. As each vehicle passed and speeded up, our driver maintained a cautious but steady speed. He waved to another bus driver traveling north in the opposite direction on her way to drop off high-school students. He had driven the route many times.

"A little late this morning," he commented.

We merged onto Highway 99 and eventually to Interstate 5. As we climbed up onto the Grapevine, we were passed up by two Kern County school buses that had been traveling with us since Bakersfield. "They have those new engines," he said, laughing. "No problems getting up this ridge Watch how they fly past us," he smiled.

A few minutes later, he spotted the stranded buses and was on his intercom phone, "Do you need any help?"

"No, just an overheated engine. Need some water and time to cool off," they answered. We continued on, arrived with plenty of time to spare, and all of us had a great tour of the library, including our bus driver. On our way back, we stopped at a fast food restaurant so that the children could use the restrooms and buy some snacks. As what usually happens on one of these trips, one of the children didn't have any money. I told her I would gladly order her something, but she'd have to wait a few moments while I organized the others into lines. I became distracted and had to look after a girl who had become sick in the bathroom. In the meantime, the bus driver saw the first girl sitting with her friends with nothing to eat. He gave her ten dollars without a second thought. He had made a friend for life.

Before long, it was time to leave. We got on board the bus. Thankfully, he allowed the children to bring their snacks with them. It was 102 degrees inside the bus, and any distraction would be helpful for our trip back. "Thank you," they each told him. The other teacher and I did too.

Finally, we were back on our two lanes, Highway 65. Above the vibrations and deafeningly noise of the bus motor, I was talking loudly with the other teacher in the seat across from me. We both saw it at the same time. A red truck was passing our bus on the left side, squeezing in front of us with not a second to spare, just as a tanker truck passed us in the opposite direction in the same left lane. Anyone who travels on Highway 65 at all has experienced such a maneuver or even lost a family member or friend this way.

Our driver just smiled at our awe. He hadn't had to slam on the brakes, swerve, or move out onto the shoulder. Because he'd been watching through his mirrors and had anticipated what the truck was planning. "I saw him coming," he said. We would have missed the whole thing if we'd been looking elsewhere.

He did share one concern with us. A white van began trailing us as we turned off of Highway 65 and onto Highway 190. He'd been watching it carefully for quite a while and told us what was happening. He had moved the bus over to the right lane several times and slowed down so that the van could pass; but instead, it just drove in closer behind the bus, too close. He returned to the left lane and the van followed, again too close. He was giving us this information in case something happened.

Finally, the van continued east on 190 as we turned left onto Plano Ave. We all let out a sigh of relief. A few minutes later, we were back at school. The children all thanked him especially for letting them eat on the bus. I said, "Thank you for getting us back safely."

Sometimes, Jesus sends strangers into our lives to safeguard us; often, these are times when we don't realize that we need help. He sends those with skills and experiences from all walks of life to help us. They usually aren't wealthy or famous but just ordinary, everyday people, and if we blink or look the other way, we just might miss the whole thing. It's how Jesus works. He's got our backside.

Ann Marie Bezayiff

Do not let your hearts be troubled. Trust in God, trust also in me.

John 14:1

And we know that in all things God works for the good of those who love him, who have been called according to his purpose

Romans 8:28

IT TAKES A WHOLE VILLAGE TO GIVE A BRIDAL SHOWER

When our daughter, Emily, announced her engagement last year, I began thinking about a wedding shower for her. She had decided to have the wedding ceremony on the East Coast where she lives instead of California. That meant that many of her family members and friends wouldn't be able to attend, which led to many conversations on how to best include them. The bridal shower was the answer.

Over the next several months, the plans were discussed and finalized. The invitations were addressed and mailed, and the menu was decided. Emily would fly out for the weekend in the spring. My sister, Carla, had offered her home, which was closer to where most of our family lives. She had the arduous task of cleaning the house and organizing the tables and chairs. Both of us searched our closets for carefully-stored linens for the tables, and we found glassware in the back spaces of our hutches. Carla found a stack of glass plates that she had almost forgotten. Emily's cousin, Nicole, organized the games and set up a chocolate fountain. Lorraine offered to bake her wonderful, homemade cookies with apricot and walnut fillings. Auntie Patty had come a day early from the coast to help us organize and set up the room arrangement the night before. She calmly put together the salads as the last details were completed and everything fell into place. Aunt Rhonda brought cupcakes with chocolate-foiled hearts and buttery croissants for each setting. Her arrangement of flowers for the centerpieces finished the tables.

The guys helped out too. They moved the furniture, set up the tables and chairs, and made those last-minute errands to the stores. David put together some awesome centerpieces for the main tables. Then they quietly disappeared just before the shower began. My brother, Jim, had arranged for a golf game that afternoon.

The guests arrived and were happy to see Emily. They had been her neighbors growing up; others were cousins and relatives. Several of her college friends had traveled from all over the state to be here. The shower was a success. Emily was so happy to see her friends and family and share this precious time together. "I feel so loved," she hugged me.

"You are," I answered.

Sometimes, we need a whole village around us to realize how much we are loved. It is in those special moments that we come to realize how much we're loved by our families and friends. Still, even as much as they love us, it is only a tiny reflection of how much Christ loves us. His love overflows even a village. It fills the earth and everything in it.

Your love, O LORD reaches to the heavens, your faithfulness to the skies.

Psalm 36:5

LADY ROSE

I looked at my sister and said, "When did Mom become so particular?"

We were shuffling stacks of clothes from the dressing room to the floor. It had taken her an hour to pick out the few items that she was now trying on. None of them were acceptable. She told us that the sleeve length was too long, the color was off, or the style wasn't right. Finally, we started pulling items off the rack. We were looking for anything that she might like, but that was even worse. "Too expensive, wrong fit, too fancy," she kept telling us. We finally gave up. "How about some lunch?" Carla and I asked at the same time.

Our parents raised us on Dad's single income, allowing our mother to be a stay-at-home mom. She had been trained as a nurse, and at rare times, she had taken an evening job to help support the family. She had never been particular or choosy when it came to her clothing or needs. Times had changed.

Sometimes, on a long weekend, my sister would drive in from Fresno and spend the night at our home. She would pick up our mom in Sanger and make a loop catching Highway 99 in Kingsburg and then to Highway 137. We had one such visit shortly after this last shopping fiasco. That afternoon, we walked downtown Porterville, walking in and out of shops. We stopped in front of a store called the Lady Rose. "I like that blouse," my mom said, pointing at the mannequin staring out at us in the window. My sister and I just looked at each other and almost pushed Mom into the store. Inside, a woman greeted us.

"Can I help you?" She asked.

"Oh, yes," we both answered at the same time.

"Well, I'm not sure," Mom said. Immediately, Carla and I began the charge.

Meanwhile, this courteous and patient woman worked around us and began talking with our mom. She began suggesting this size, another color, or that style. She even offered to have the alterations done by someone she knew. "Your daughter can pick them up when they're ready," she offered.

We left less than an hour later with several outfits and matching earrings too. After that day, whenever my mom came to visit, we would beat a path to the Lady Rose. My mom always enjoyed shopping there and always came away with some very nice outfits. This was our tradition for several years. Then, just before Christmas of 2006, my mother passed on. After working through all the arrangements, the funeral, and getting her house ready to sell, I found myself walking past the Lady Rose on a brisk winter day. However, the Lady Rose was closed. It had passed on too. I thought to myself, *I wonder if I will ever cross paths with the owner. I wish I could thank her for everything she'd done for my mom.* I smiled to myself. *And for my sister and me.*

Above all, love each other deeply, because love covers over a multitude of sins. Offer hospitality to one another without grumbling. Each one should use whatever gift he has received to serve others, faithfully administering God's grace in its various forms.

1 Peter 4:8–10

RAINSTORM AND CRAB CAKES

Our daughter's wedding was over a week away. David and I had decided to take a break from all the last-minute planning and take a trip over to St. Michaels on the eastern shore of Maryland. We left Emily's apartment early one morning and drove toward the Bay Bridge to cross over to our destination. Soon, we found ourselves driving over an incredible bridge. The view of Chesapeake Bay below us was spectacular. Sailboats crisscrossed underneath us like tiny white matchsticks. Barges were towing larger ships, and motor boats of all descriptions displayed their power and force as they hustled in and out of each other's way. Too soon we were on the other side of the bridge but we were not disappointed. The land there was lush and green, estuaries and inlets dotting the landscape everywhere we looked.

We arrived at St. Michaels and took Talbot Street to the end of the town before turning back and finally found a room for the night. The town appeared to be resting after the busy summer weekend. The crowd at the Crab Claw had disappeared, and we shared a quiet dinner overlooking the bay. The next day, we enjoyed our role as tourists and had planned to take a day cruise. We never made it. Black clouds began forming and threatened a fierce thunderstorm before we were half-way to the dock. So we turned back into town instead. We soon found ourselves drenched from the rainstorm and began looking for cover and maybe an early dinner as well.

The only place that was opened was the Chesapeake Saloon. We headed inside and found the place filled with the locals—the people who lived and worked nearby. The place was vibrant and alive. Customers and bartenders were discussing their jobs, while a splatter-ing of jokes and antidotes mixed in to create a boom of laughter now and then. We found a table next to a group of young women who were busy talking about their hectic day, while sampling each other's appetizers. We slipped into our seats sand ordered a drink. Already, I felt warmer and a little drier.

We spotted a door on our left that said, "Restaurant." David investigated and discovered that it was open. We found ourselves seated in a room empty of customers except for ourselves. Carved wooden benches marked out the tables and pictures of sailing vessels, and local history filled the walls.

I ordered the crab cakes. What else would you order in a restaurant on the Eastern Shore? As we waited for our meal, we began to talk about our children and the upcoming marriage, but our conversation shifted to our own life together, our courtship, and our own rain-soaked wedding, our travels, and our adventures. We relived funny antidotes and glossed over disappoint-ments that we had shared. We realized that things hadn't always worked out the way we had planned, but then, we added, something else always seemed to have come along to balance the disappointments—sometimes different, sometimes unexpected, and most times, better.

Soon, our private reflections, our life together, and our conversations seemed to fill the empty room with life, as loudly as if a thousand people had been sharing with us. We didn't have to say more than a few words to each other to understand the moment we were sharing.

Then out came the crab cakes. I asked the server, "Just what goes into making a crab cake? Is there a recipe?"

"Oh, no, can't tell you that." She looked at me in real surprise. "Each cook has his own recipe. Some put in more filler; maybe bread crumbs or mayonnaise, but the good ones have plenty of crab. That's all I can tell you. No recipe, just what's in your head and plenty of practice." She added as an afterthought, "And your own secret ingredients."

I laughed. Just like marriage. I winked at David. Each couple has to come up with their own recipe. Some turn out better than others. In another week, our daughter and future son-in-law would be starting their own life together, making their own recipe. I know that God will be in the mix.

Just then the rain stopped. We finished our meal and got back to our room just before another cloud burst. Even when unexpected, rain can be such a blessing.

> I will bless them and the places surround my hill. I will send down the showers in season; there will be showers of blessings.
>
> Ezekiel 34:26

ARE YOU LISTENING?

My car and I retired this year. This wasn't any ordinary car. It was my traveling companion, administrative center on wheels, and extended classroom. The back hatch was perfect for loading and unloading. It had hauled boxed sack lunches and crates of milk from the district kitchen for field trips. There were props and sports equipment, CDs, boxes of supplies for each new school year, salads and pastries for staff treats and potlucks. At the end of each week, it transported stacks of papers and tests to my home to correct and return on Mondays.

I was relieved that it had lasted until the end of the year. This gave us time to read up on automobile reports, do some Internet searches, and visit dealerships. We made our list and started with the same make and model of my current car. Upon arriving at the dealership, we were escorted to a salesman who proceeded to show me a newer, larger version of my car. "That's too big," I told him.

"Look how great this is for kids," he answered and began pulling down seats.

"I don't have any kids at home. They're grown," I told him. Ignoring me, he continued to show me all the features and repeated at least four more times how great it is for kids.

I was flattered that he thought I was young enough to have small children at home—or was it a marketing ploy? I was annoyed. He wasn't listening.

Finally, he asked me, "What color do you like?"

"I haven't thought of a color yet, but maybe gray, silver." Within five minutes, an even larger car appeared on the showroom floor. It was silver. Nice that he at least heard that. We left.

Are you a good listener? Many people identify with the Christian faith. They were raised in Christian churches, attended services and Sunday school, but don't attend any church today. What are their reasons? Do we take the time to ask that question? What are their disappointments, hurts, and concerns when it comes to churches? Do we create an honest, open dialogue? Do we take the time to listen, really listen? I've had a repairman witness to me when he should have been repairing my refrigerator. "Yes, I'm a Christian. Can you fix the refrigerator now?" But he continued his witnessing. Then there was the public employee who was supposed to help me with some legal papers. He managed to throw in his experiences as a Christian. "Yes, that's great." I agreed, "I'm a Christian too. Can we finish with the paper work?" But he continued on with his programmed dialogue. "Do I look like I need saving right now?" He didn't think that was funny.

Yes, Christians are told in Mark 16:15 that they are to share the good news with all creation. But in James 1:19 it also tells us to be quick to listen, slow to speak.

Eventually, we found a car that better suited my new status as retired teacher. It's much smaller and gets better gas mileage. Part of the deal was an exceptional trade-in price. It was more than my car was really worth. So I left my companion on the back lot with all the other trade-ins. They were waiting patiently in silent rows, ready to be picked up for some car auction or sold for parts. It was difficult to say good-bye, but my new car was waiting. I understood that Christ had a new plan for my life, but I also realized that I would need to work on my listening skills for directions.

> He said to them, "Go into all the world and preach the good news to all creation."
>
> Mark 16:15

> My dear brothers, take note of this: Everyone should be quick to listen, slow to speak...
>
> James 1:19

FLORA-BAMA: FINDING GOD'S PEACE IN THE MIDST OF DESTRUCTION

There's a building standing on both sides of the Florida-Alabama border called the Flora-Bama. It grew up piecemeal on a beach front between the two states. The Alabama side has since been sold to the high-rise building next door, but the name remains. The place is a collection of shanty-like buildings connected to each other with wooden overhangs and unleveled flooring. Autographs of the famous and not-so-famous are etched into walls, furniture, and doors everywhere. A beautiful white sandy beach is its back porch. The surroundings scream "party time" with three separate stages open for bands and musicians and discarded swimsuit tops hanging from the rafters. We arrived around noon so we didn't get the chance to experience the evening bash. We were on our way to Houston to visit our son. This was one of those side trips to remember, but not because of its party atmosphere.

Even though the place was open, it was quiet with only a few people around. In one of the rooms, a small group of people were sitting at a table having drinks. It was already very hot, and we were thirsty so we ordered bottled water from the woman tending the bar. We began a conversation. The oil spill was fresh on everyone's mind. Tourists were staying away; beaches were empty. This part of the gulf coast was facing severe economic problems. "As bad as this is, it doesn't compare to Hurricane Ivan. This isn't anything that we won't survive," she told us. "I lost everything to that hurricane.

"We were told to evacuate, but I wasn't going anywhere. My two sons sent their girlfriends to pick me up. So I packed a couple of things, thinking I would be back in a few days. When I called my sons to pick me up, they told me there wasn't anything left of my home. I didn't believe them. Told them I had their number. They just wanted to use my house for a party. They did that to me before. But my son tells me there's nothing left. Nothing left. Well, I found my way back home. My son was right. No party; just broken windows and collapsed walls all over the place." She stopped for a minute. "Everything was gone. Everything was gone except for a pole, like one of those wooden telephone poles, standing right in front of where my kitchen window used to be. An osprey lived there. It's protected; so we couldn't remove the pole, ugly as it was. Wouldn't you know it; that osprey was sitting on that pole just like when I left." She laughed. "An endangered bird managed to survive Ivan, but my house was destroyed."

She finished, "If that ole bird could survive, I knew I would too. God put that in my heart."

As we were talking, an additional crew of workers arrived, and slowly, the place came to life. We walked around the buildings and onto the beach. High-rise apartments and hotels provided a backdrop for the few tourists basking in the hot sun. Children with their plastic buckets were few and far between. Black globs of unprocessed oil dotted the landscape as the waves deposited its poisonous stash. Not a pretty sight.

We ended up ordering shrimp baskets and fries with sweet tea. This wasn't a place to count calories or worry over cholesterol levels. A cold beer would have been great, but we still had a lot of driving to do. Too soon, we were back on the road heading back to I-10. I took away with me a story of survival and the paradigm of God's peace in the midst of destruction.

> Rejoice in the Lord always. I will say it again: Rejoice! Do not be anxious about anything, but in everything, by prayer and petition, with thanksgiving, present your requests to God. And the peace of God, which transcends all understanding, will guard your hearts and your minds in Christ Jesus.
>
> Philippians 4:4, 6–7

PEOPLE OF GOD THROWN ON THE FRONT LINES

"Mom," Emily spoke over the phone. "I just got a call from Brian. He's locked in an office on the third floor. There's a shooter in the building." Silence. "We need prayer."

Later, he told us that it was the dinging sound of the elevator doors opening and closing that was the most unnerving. A second phone call from Emily informed us that both Brian and his brother had been evacuated from the building. After a four-hour stand-off, a trained marksman shot and killed the explosive strapped shooter before he could fire his guns at the three hostages in the lobby.

As I called family and friends asking for prayer, I learned that our sister-in-law's granddaughter had broken her arm in several places, and they were at Children's Hospital in Madera. A fourth grader in my sister's school lost control in class and began throwing furniture at the other students and the teacher. The principal and vice principal called the police but not before their arms and legs were badly bruised after trying to restrain the child.

Less than a week before, a Mormon bishop had been shot in Visalia. "I need to talk to the man in charge of the church," the shooter said. When he appeared, the bishop was shot to death; the gunman didn't know his name. The motive? No one will ever know because the shooter killed himself with the same gun.

A string of diagnoses of cancer, tumors, and other medical problems poured over the e-mail prayer chain.

Here are people of God thrown on the front lines.

These are merely a small list of examples; each one of us has our own list of difficulties and contradictions we experience personally or read about every day.

Years ago, after a string of well-known ministers and evangelists confessed publically to adulterous affairs and encounters, I remember asking my brother, Rich, "Why do you think this happening?"

His response was, "It's a war, a spiritual war. Ministers, priests, spiritual leaders, all of them are on the front lines; fighting temptation thrown at them constantly, every day. Christians are always under attack, but the leaders more so." His words came back to me as I thought over the events of the past weeks.

We may be under attack, but do not fear. His love is woven into our armor. Our weapons are prayer, and our strength comes from God.

> So do not fear, for I am with you, do not be dismayed, for I am your God. I will strengthen you and help you; I will uphold you with my righteous right hand.
>
> Isaiah 41:10

PROTECTING
THE HARVEST

I heard the dull rhythmic thud of olives filing empty buckets. The pickers had arrived! I stepped outside, and although it was past midmorning, a cool rush of autumn air pushed against my face. Workers were straddled on ladders, pushing their bodies into the olive-laden branches. Their uniforms—long pants and shirts, caps, and cotton gloves—protected them from sharp leaves, webs, loose debris, and stain from their chore. A man called out something in Spanish and was answered with a song. Others joined in, but then a quiet settled over the trees. Only the rustle of people's hands weaving their way in and out of tree branches and the thump of olives continued. Then a male voice rose up above the trees, a serenade to a lost love, and then the quiet thudding again.

By the end of the day's picking, we stared in unbelief at the five-hundred-pound bins filled with our olives. We couldn't believe this unexpected windfall. This would be a real harvest. In past seasons, buyers wouldn't accept our olives because we owned fewer than ten acres. Some years we sold olives to small local companies that pressed olives for oil. By the time the pickers were paid, little, if any, profit was left, but at least the trees had been picked. In our naïveté and inexperience, one contractor kept most of the profits for his picking costs. Then there were years when the trees hadn't produced.

In spite of everything, we had taken care of our trees. Branches and suckers had been pruned, the cuttings shredded, irrigation lines were set down and replaced, trees and weeds sprayed, and upkeep on the well and the pump along with orders for irrigation water continued.

The picking continued the next day, and the number of filled bins was beyond our expectations. The contractor was pleased at the amount but also with the quality of the fruit from our trees.

"Now watch those bins," he told us after the day's picking. "Those guys working the fields across the street will steal them from right under your nose. They can load your bins and be gone before you know it. Our truck should be here later on."

So I dragged a folding chair out into the field and sat next to our bins. I stayed there until their flatbed truck drove away and the forklift was parked. I went inside to work on a weaving project, but after about ten minutes, I heard another truck pull up in front of our bins; someone started a forklift. I opened the door and heard human bird whistles and calls warning the driver. The forklift was already on our access road next to where our bins rested, but then the driver quickly turned his forklift around and returned across the street. I dragged out my folding chair and sat next to the bins until the forklift had been parked again and the truck pulled away. When they finally drove away, the driver waved at me and I waved back. I was still working the harvest.

> Then another angel came out of the temple and called in a loud voice to him who was sitting on the cloud, "Take your sickle and reap, because the time to reap has come, for the harvest of the earth is ripe." So he who was seated on the cloud swung his sickle over the earth, and the earth was harvested.
>
> Revelation 14:15–16

HOPE FOR THE SMALLEST OF HARVESTS

A week later, the contractor came by to pick up his check. David met him at the front door. They exchanged a few words while an older man emerged from the parked car and joined them.

"Thank you for the work." He shook David's hand.

"Thank you for picking our olives," David answered. "We didn't think anyone would want to pick for us because we're so small."

"No, thank you for the work. My son here is getting his contractor's license next month. I always tell him to take any job, big or small. The size of the job doesn't matter; it's having work that matters. We appreciate the work. When the fruit is ready, we work. Saturday and Sunday, we work because the harvest is ready. "

So we continue working and preparing for the harvest in our own lives, in our jobs, with family relationships, in our communities, and our spiritual life, knowing that the work of any harvest is never finished.

We give thanks for the harvest, the workers in the fields, and God, who ripens the fruit. We who believe are the Lord's harvest, and the good fruit of our lives is his glory.

> Let us not become weary in doing good, for at the proper time we will reap a harvest if we do not give up.
>
> Galatians 6:9

GRANDPARENTS RAISING GRANDCHILDREN

I met Sara, my neighbor, in front of my country drive-way and we walked four miles today. She carried a wooden dowel with her to chase away stray dogs. We passed by olive and orange orchards, barking dogs, and sidestepped cars and school buses on two-lane coun-try roads. We passed a field of workers cutting swollen bunches of purple grapes from vines. Along the edge of the road, other workers stood in front of makeshift platforms, packing bunches into cardboard boxes for shipping. Flatbed trucks lined both sides of the road waiting for their loads. It was early and still cool. A few workers nodded their heads as we passed by. "*Buenos dias,*" they said. The fresh aroma of squashed grapes mixed with powdery dust met us and brought back familiar childhood smells.

On our first walk together, Sara pointed out a rustic wooden house, the front surrounded with an enclosed screen porch. Its walls looked shaky and in need of paint, but Jessica and her husband have lived there many years—a benefit of his job. Now, their grandchil-dren live with them as well. A couple of years ago, their daughter disappeared without warning and left behind the children—four of them with ages ranging from two to eight years old. Only two of the children had the same father, and none of the fathers were around. Jessica's daughter had been on drugs. She had tried many times to break the addiction and become a good mother, but it was too much. So she left, vanished.

The grandparents took the children into their home; however, because they lacked written documentation that the mother had left them in their care, they couldn't get medical help for them. There was also the problem of enrolling them into a new school. Birth certificates and immunization records were buried in the mess left behind. Even though the grandfather had a job, he didn't make enough money to cover the additional cost of food and clothing for the children. The stress was too much; he had a heart attack and then a stroke. Jessica had to divide her time between the children and his medical needs. He couldn't work for months, and Jessica had no one to turn to for help.

This is when Sara, on one of her walks, first met Jessica. Jessica shared her story while Sara listened. As Jessica continued to work through the process of gaining custody of the children and caring for her husband, Sara got food, clothing, and other necessities for the family through her church, family, and friends.

After months of paperwork, phone calls, and legal formalities, Jessica and her husband received custody of the children and became eligible for financial help. In time, Jessica's husband returned to work but even with limited help from the county; there wasn't enough for anything but the basics. Sara continued to look out after them, checking in on Jessica at least once a week during her walks. Her church continued to provide food and other needed supplies.

In the darkest hour, a light emerged. It was Sara. But it wasn't just Sara. Sara was the messenger. The light came from all of us. It came from everyone who has ever donated money, food, time or gift cards. It came from those who gave but never knew why or saw the fruits of their giving. It was everyone praying for grandparents raising grandchildren, parents lost to drug addiction, and the children who grow up in such turmoil. In our hearts God has woven the desire to care for others; no matter the circumstances. In our hearts God has woven a desire to do good works.

> For we are God's workmanship, created in Christ Jesus to do good works, which God prepared in advance for us to do.
>
> Ephesians 2:10

Afterword

Eventually, the children's mother was caught with drugs and incarcerated but not before she became pregnant with another child. Unfortunately, this is not an uncommon story. It's the time and place we live in; however, the story is not finished because with Christ all things are possible. So we continue to do good works in his name.

HANDWEAVER'S SHOW

The members of our local handweavers' guild held their annual sale again this year in Exeter. As I entered the front door, my eyes went on hyperactive overdrive with all the colors and combinations of fabrics and yarns. I felt my credit card tremble. Tables had been lined up and were completely covered with an array of items for sale. Felted hats and bags, towels, coasters, baby blankets, tapestry rugs, hand-dyed yarns, and so much more were piled high. Also, a few individual vendors had set up their makeshift booths offering even more yarns and various hand-working products. I had thought of selling some of my own kitchen towels and a few shawls that I had woven but had given most of them as way as gifts. *Maybe next year*, I thought. It was always next year. The idea of someone actually paying money for my work was unnerving.

Interspersed among the tables were guild members taking turns demonstrating their skills on floor, table, and inkle looms. Others worked at the spinning wheels, pulling out bits of wool stuffed in oversized plastic bags and magically transforming them into uniform strands of yarn for knitting, crocheting, or weaving.

My favorite section has always been the clothing. I went directly to that area, where bags, jackets, dresses, shawls, and vests flowed from artistic displays. The workmanship was outstanding, each a piece of authentic clothing art. I always wanted to ask one of the artists how they managed to overcome that first cut into the cloth but thought better of showing my insecurities and lack of confidence.

Even though I had started numerous projects with the intent to create a piece of clothing on my own, when the time actually came, the scissors froze in my hands. I couldn't force myself to cut up the cloth that had taken me days of work. Even though I had taken clothing construction classes, read magazines, talked with other weavers, and bought several books with patterns, I was never ready to take the next step. So until I do, I will continue with my towels and shawls. Not that towels and shawls haven't been rewarding and challenging, but I know I need to take my skill to the next level. Maybe the next project would be the one.

In developing our relationship with Christ, we need to take the next step. Reading the Bible, prayer, fellowship, worship, and study are necessary, wonderful avenues. However, if these are merely activities, substitutes for the busyness of the world, we can't really hear what God is trying to say to us.

Finding the quiet spaces in our lives for meditation and introspection is difficult. It's unnatural in our fast-paced world but, when we make the time to sit quietly and listen, we can find that small still voice of God inside. Finding the time for these holy leave of absences, these short spiritual getaways, is indispensable in our walk with God.

Then a great and powerful wind tore the mountains apart and shattered the rocks before the LORD, but the LORD was not in the wind. After the wind there was an earthquake, but the LORD was not in the earthquake. After the earthquake came a fire, but the LORD was not in the fire. And after the fire came a gentle whisper.

1 Kings 19:11–13

WEAVING A LEGACY: EXIT RIGHT

The test was over. The last child closed her test booklet. Stone silence followed me as I collected the answer documents and test booklets. Carefully and slowly, I piled them on the counter, turned toward the thirty pair of eyes watching me intently, and said, "We're finished." The release from the children was no more dramatic than a volcanic explosion. The pressure was off! With loud and expressive voices, they all started talking at once. "Line up; early recess," I stated. "Grab your snack as you leave." They ran down the corridor until I reminded them to walk—they still ran.

"No more "rock the test." One of the children laughed as I locked the door and we followed the students to the playground together.

"No more "rock the test." I laughed. Every morning for the last month, we had recited those words over the intercom. "Who's the best? We are. We will, we will rock the test."

The past month had been difficult to say the least. At first, the staff couldn't understand the numerous complaints of stomachaches, throwing up during the school day, and the creative inventions of illnesses that allowed them to go home early. Students lacked their normal patience and tolerance for each other. Fighting and name-calling occurred daily, ending with bruised egos, scratches, and in the worse cases, suspension. He-said-she-said gossiping intensified among the girls, ending many friendships. Some of the more fragile students began a systematic shutdown, and a few sat with a stubborn immobility. Homework wasn't getting done. Classroom assignments were incomplete and poorly done. We quickly realized the anticipation and pressure to do well on the test was negatively affecting our students. We tried to soften the reality of the test as much as possible. However, the importance of the test and the children's scores could not be downplayed. So much was riding on those scores.

As I watched the children playing on the field, I sensed their relief and I felt myself relax. As the other classes joined us, the playground filled with laughing and playing sounds. I laughed for no reason.

As we lined up to return to class, a student came up to me and shared his disappointment. He didn't get into the charter school for next year, even though it was located four blocks from his home. "I didn't get in. Test scores. You know, all my problems."

"That's okay," I said. "This is your school. You have a place here next year."

The next two weeks were filled with end-of-the-year activities, including science projects and a visit to a presidential library. They earned an afternoon swim party at the local public pool and ate pizza and made ice cream sundaes for our un-birthday party. We read a novel together. For the last few days of school, the children learned to play softball and autographed each other's good citizenship t-shirts and memory books. Then, on the last day, with much emotion and some tears, the entire school said good-bye to the sixth graders. They were off to junior high school after a promotion ceremony in the cafeteria that morning. Finally, all that was left was to distribute the infamous report card. There were lots of hugs and much excitement—the school year was over.

With emotion, I said good-bye too. I had decided to retire. This was my last day of teaching after a lifetime of working with students. Along with lessons in reading, writing, and math, I had tried to instill a love for learning into my students, to scratch that itch of curiosity with investigation and meet challenges with confidence and knowledge. I never told them they could become anything they wanted. Life doesn't always work that way. But with hard work and discipline, the door of opportunity would open. The odds were they'd never become professional athletes, but sports could be a part of their lives. The fame and wealth that comes from being a rock star might elude them, but learning a musical instrument or singing in a choir were real possibilities. Most wouldn't impact the world as Mother Theresa, but each could make a difference in neighborhoods and communities where they lived. I taught them to be cautious of "homies," those so-called friends selling drugs, alcohol, and cigarettes, thereby making money off their bodies; those precious bodies that God created needed to last them an entire lifetime.

I picked up one last box off the top of my desk but set it back down as an old lesson plan book fell out and onto the floor. A piece of paper wiggled its way out. I replaced the planning book back into the box while picking up the paper and began reading. They were goals I had written years ago: educating the whole child, planting seeds of faith and encouragement, enjoyment in reading, and recognizing the possibilities in life. These were idealist, lofty, and not measurable in today's world of statistics and data-driven instruction. I folded the paper and pushed it into my pocket. These goals, written so long ago, were my goals now; I claimed them for the next stage of my life. As I headed toward the door, I looked back over the classroom and realized that my students had shaped me. Education goes both ways. I said one last prayer over the room and closed the door behind me. My legacy was woven. Music filled my head, a dancing tune. I hummed it out loud as it swirled inside my head. I picked up my box, danced into the parking lot, and made my exit, right into my car.

My piece is woven. It is finished, and I am pleased with the outcome. The threads of yarn are tightly woven and the salvages are as even as any I have woven in the past. The pattern is unique, not quite like I had envisioned, but close enough. The colors are perfect together and create a unity that I couldn't have envisioned. I have fringed the ends and washed the shawl. It is soft. The work is done. I am satisfied. So tomorrow, I will begin a new piece.

> Forget the former things, do not dwell on the past. See, I am doing a new thing! Now it springs up; do you not perceive it? I am making a way in the desert and streams in the wasteland.
>
> Isaiah 43:18–19

CONCLUSION

He has filled them with skill to do all kinds of
work as craftsmen, designers, embroiderers in blue,
purple and scarlet yarn and fine linen, and weavers—all of them master craftsmen and designers.

Exodus 35:35

RESOURCES

Wilder, Laura Ingalls, *The First Four Years*, Harper and Row, Publishers, NY, Copyright 1971

Zochert, Donald, *Laura, the Life of Laura Ingalls Wilder*, Henry Regnery Company, Chicago, Ill, 60601, Copyright 1976